A Christian Approach to Political Decision-Making

A Christian Approach to Political Decision-Making

Introducing Whisper Ethics

RICK HERRICK

WIPF & STOCK · Eugene, Oregon

A CHRISTIAN APPROACH TO POLITICAL DECISION MAKING
Introducing Whisper Ethics

Wipf & Stock
An Imprint of Wipf and Stock Publishers
199 W. 8th Ave., Suite 3
Eugene, OR 97401

www.wipfandstock.com

PAPERBACK ISBN: 979-8-3852-0353-6
HARDCOVER ISBN: 979-8-3852-0354-3
EBOOK ISBN: 979-8-3852-0355-0

VERSION NUMBER 11/15/23

For Dave, with profound gratitude

Contents

Acknowledgments

A Christian Approach to Political Decision-Making: Introducing Whisper Ethics culminates more than fifty years of thinking about these issues as a trained political scientist and a committed Christian. I have one large debt to acknowledge in writing this book.

David Kranz is a skeptic when it comes to religion and was a distinguished English professor at Dickinson College. He applied his mind as a skeptic to significantly improve the theoretical part of the book in Chapter 1, and his English professor's training was in evidence throughout to make the text read more smoothly.

Even more important to me as a person, Dave has been my close friend for sixty years. We have competed against each other in sports and spent many nights drinking wine while discussing philosophy or solving the political problems confronting our nation and the world.

The most important character trait defining Dave is kindness. While not believing in much that the book claims about Whisper Ethics, he spent hours working with me to make the central thesis governing the book clear on my terms and not his. You can't ask more of a friend. It is for this reason I am honored to dedicate the book to him.

Finally, I want to thank the Wipf and Stock staff for their friendly cooperation in putting this project together and for their considerable help with editing the final draft. The speed at which they work to accomplish each task in the publication process is impressive. I have worked with five publishing houses, and this group is in a league of their own.

Introduction

THERE HAS BEEN A central focus for my life that goes back as long as I can remember. I have wanted to live the teachings of Jesus. My journey toward this goal has been a long one with many fits and starts, but after sixty years of focus on the problem, I have come to some answers which you may find helpful if you have similar ambitions. This book will demonstrate how Christians make political decisions; and, more importantly, it will provide tools to suggest ways Christians can do a better job living Jesus' teachings.

I began my journey as most Christians do—with prayer. I asked God, my Father in heaven, to make me into a new creation. I got this idea from writing my honor's thesis in college on Paul's letter to the Romans. In chapter 13:3, Paul calls on his followers to model their behavior in the world on a transformed mind.

I asked God to transform my mind so that I could live in the world in a new way, a way that served my neighbor and directed me away from self-centered concerns. It didn't work. God never answered that prayer. Over time I came to think differently about God. The father in heaven who answers our prayers made less and less sense. Reflecting on the Holocaust, where six million Jews who prayed to the same God I do were sent to their deaths, reinforced this new thinking about prayer. In Chapter 1, I will present ideas that inform my new thinking about the nature of God and how this force for goodness and love works in the world.

Most Protestant Christians take their cues from the Bible when thinking about the relation between religion and politics. I tried that approach too, but, again, I found this solution to my problem of living the teachings of Jesus to be lacking. There are several problems with it.

The first is that the New Testament is a very human book, written by first-century authors who had differing opinions as to who Jesus was. With the Gospels presenting four different pictures of the historical Jesus, you can find a passage in the New Testament to support any political position you choose to take. This problem can be readily seen if we compare two contemporary writers in the field.

Wayne Grudem is the author of *Politics According to the Bible*. According to Grudem, God intended the Bible to give guidance in every area of life, including politics.[1] His book could have been written by a staff member of the Republican National Committee or the Trump White House. Grudem finds a biblical passage to support small government, school choice, lower taxes, a strong military, greatly reduced government regulation, an out-of-control Environmental Protection Agency, and the absolute right to own a gun.

Jim Wallis, another passage picker, comes to very different conclusions. In *God's Politics: Why the Right Gets It Wrong*, Wallis cites Christian scripture to support nuclear disarmament and the massive transfer of wealth to poorer nations. He supports responsible gun control legislation and policies to reduce economic inequality in the United States, as well as policies to combat racism. His politics reflect the Bernie Sanders wing of the Democratic party with a biblical passage to support each position taken.

Let's briefly look at the positions of the two writers on the role of government in the economy. Grudem argues the teachings of the Bible support private ownership, free market capitalism, and limited, at best, government regulation. He cites Gen 1:28 to suggest that God wants economic growth. Private property is sacred, as is seen in the seventh commandment "you shall not steal" (Exod 20:15). Because we are created in God's image (Gen 1:27), God

1. Grudem, *Politics According to the Bible*, 13.

wants us to be like him. When we own private property, we reflect his glory.[2]

In contrast, Jim Wallis points out there are several thousand passages in the Bible calling for economic justice and support for the poor.[3] He cites passages in Isaiah and Micah promoting economic justice. The psalms, according to Wallis, are all about defending the oppressed. Leviticus calls for freeing slaves, forgiving debt, and redistributing land. In the New Testament, the Beatitudes bless the poor, and Matt 25:31–41 blesses those who help the poor. The teachings of Jesus are all about economic justice and the dangers of excessive wealth accumulation. As this brief comparison suggests, the two writers find biblical passages to support the contrasting political positions they take.

When we move away from passage picking and consider the big picture, problems persist. The Old Testament is a mixed blessing. You see deep concern for the poor, the marginalized, and a preference for solving disputes with nonviolence throughout. On the other hand, you find support for slavery, and women are considered to be second-class citizens.

Read about Joshua at Jericho. When the walls came tumbling down, Joshua and his troops enter and carry out God's orders to slaughter all residents in the town—men, women, and children. God gave a similar order to Moses to exact his vengeance against the Midianites (See Num 31: 1–12). Even the prophets reveal a God of anger and vengeance when it comes to people in Israel who displease him by worshiping multiple gods or by practicing rituals that miss the point. See Amos 3:2 and 3:11; Hos 2:2–7 and 13:7–8; Isa 3: 1–9; Jer 5:7–17; and Ezek 11:6–12.

Many Christians believe the God of the New Testament is different, that the God of anger and vengeance has become the God of love and forgiveness. Bart Ehrman asks the obvious question: did God change?[4] Sadly, the answer is no. Yes, there are the teach-

2. This is just the tip of the iceberg. See chapter 9 in his book for a full listing of the biblical passages supporting free market capitalism.

3. See Wallis, *God's Politics*, 209–22.

4. Ehrman, *Armageddon*, 143.

ings of Jesus calling for economic and social justice, inclusion, and the practice of nonviolence. And yet slavery is still supported, and women remain second-class citizens in several letters alleged to be written by Paul and others.

The message of the book of Revelation is shocking.[5] It is all about the wrath and vengeance of a very angry God. This God inflicts horrible suffering on the planet. At the final judgment, all those who have lived will be brought back to life. Those who displeased God, which will include most of us, will be thrown into a lake of burning sulfur so that we can suffer eternally. Paul suggests a similar fate for nonbelievers in 1 Thess 5:3. According to Matthew, nonbelievers will be dealt with like the victims of Noah's flood (Matt 24: 37–38).

What most Christians don't recognize is that salvation is only for a small group of people. You see this emphasis throughout the New Testament, but let me draw your attention to what I consider to be a significant problem. The expectation emerged among the followers of Jesus that belief in Jesus Christ as the Messiah would bring salvation in heaven. The resurrection proved this belief for many of these close followers. If this is true, why were there so few witnesses to the resurrection—only the disciples and a few women were granted such an opportunity. Peter gives this rather dirty little secret away when he says:

> And they killed him by hanging him on a tree. Yet on the third day God raised him to life and allowed him to be seen, not by the whole people, but only by certain witnesses that God had chosen beforehand. (Acts 10:39–41)

If God is all about love, which is the God that nourishes my life, that God would have had the resurrected Jesus shake hands with every resident of Jerusalem. This would have allowed the thousands of Jews in Jerusalem for Passover an equal chance in coming to believe in Jesus as the Messiah, thus giving them eternal life in heaven according to traditional Christian belief.

5. For an excellent commentary on the book of Revelation, see Ehrman cited above.

A further problem for using the Bible as a moral compass for making political decisions as a Christian is relevance. Jesus' teachings relate to a first-century society that couldn't be more different from our world two thousand years later. When the rich man asks Jesus what he must do to enter the kingdom of heaven, Jesus tells him to "sell all your possessions, give the money to the poor, and only then can you follow me" (Matt 19:16–21, paraphrased). But that rich man had a life expectancy of thirty-five years and lived in a society which valued taking care of strangers. Followers of Jesus could expect to be provided for. Yes, serving the poor is important, but we live in a world with a much higher life expectancy which requires that we save money if we hope to live well in old age.

How does climate change relate in a direct way to the teachings of Jesus? The problem only became apparent a hundred years ago. You might say it relates to Jesus' command to serve neighbors, but the neighbors to be most affected by a changing climate have yet to be born. The Bible has nothing to say about this problem.

Because we know so little about the historical Jesus, a related problem arises pertaining to what some of his teachings mean. Are the teachings on nonviolence a timeless universal ethic or a strategy to deal with a specific first-century threat? The New Testament provides no clues as to what Jesus intended here.

Rome leveled Sephoris, a city three miles from Nazareth, a few years before Jesus was born. It's highly likely Jesus lost family members—grandparents, uncles, and aunts. It's also known that Roman soldiers were stationed in Nazareth while this slaughter was taking place. Male members of this tiny village were enslaved. Female members were forced to service Roman soldiers. These atrocities could have easily included Jesus' parents. With a vivid knowledge of this tragic chapter in the history of Nazareth, Jesus may have preached nonviolence, not as a universal ethic, but as a strategy on how best to survive Roman colonialism. God will take care of Rome. If we create loving communities, we can come to ignore Roman oppression.

The Bible inspires me. I get goose bumps when I read about the political positions taken by the prophets, Jesus, and Paul in the societies in which they lived. I pledge each day to live and act more like they did, but I don't take my cues for political decision-making from the stories in the Bible about them. The key phrase in the sentence above is "in the societies in which they lived." Because these societies were so different, religious figures in the Bible can inspire us, but they cannot provide a road map for ethical decision-making in the world today.

As the examples of Wayne Grudem and Jim Wallis suggest, passage picking is used to lend support to positions taken by suggesting that God is on their side. In addition to being an arrogant assumption, the problem is that such picking can't explain how individual Christians actually make decisions or how we can bring our politics more in line with the teachings of Jesus. This book will provide answers to both questions.

Roman Catholics use a different approach. They take their cues on applying their religion to politics from the teachings of the church—a very human institution. Again, we find a mixed record. The current Pope Francis is an inspiring figure with his passionate commitment to the poor and his support for solving the problems surrounding climate change, his concern for human rights, and his efforts to promote international peace.

On the other hand, priests remain celibate in Pope Francis's church. Is this because God thinks it's important? I can't imagine that. Until very recently the purpose of human sexuality was only for procreation. So sad! And then there's the church's continued opposition to abortion, which we will deal with in chapter two. Finally, and of most importance in highlighting this problem, there is a two-thousand-year history of anti-Semitism quietly endorsed by the church. This moral failure becomes most clear when we recognize the church failed to condemn National Socialism as it was unfolding in Germany during the 1930s and 1940s which led to the killing of six million Jews.[6]

The sad truth is that many Christians are reluctant to apply their religion to politics, and it shows. In my book *Moving Beyond*

6. *Constantine's Sword* by James Carroll provides an excellent account of this tragic history of anti-Semitism.

Belief,[7] I outline in detail the failure of the Christian church to apply Jesus' teachings to politics. While I won't repeat myself here, I will briefly summarize those findings. Over the last two thousand years, we see Christians fighting Christians all in the name of the prince of peace. We find a history of church support of anti-Semitism in Europe and discrimination in other places, such as apartheid in South Africa and slavery in the United States.

In contemporary America, there has never been a time when the teachings of Jesus have been more important. The survival of our planet requires real solutions to the problems of climate change and the ever-increasing threat posed by the spread of nuclear weapons. Our democracy is threatened by a lack of civility among the partisan players, most of whom claim to be Christian. Gun violence in our country is out of control, and the economy has never been more skewed in favor of the rich.

There are more than two billion Christians in the world, and the truth is that we have not done much to make the world a better place to live. As this brief introduction has suggested, traditional approaches to the application of the Christian religion to politics have not worked well. The purpose of this book is to introduce a new approach to the problem of applying religion to politics I call Whisper Ethics. Whisper Ethics is defined in the next chapter. It is an approach to Christian ethics that has finally enabled me to do a better job living the teachings of Jesus. Chapter 2 will apply the concept to real-world political situations in an attempt to add clarity to the outline provided in chapter 1.

A few explanatory notes are necessary before we get started. I will use traditional designations for Jewish and Christian Scriptures because I find the terms "Old Testament" and "New Testament" more specific and less likely to lead to confusion. By adopting this strategy, I do not imply in any way that Christian Scripture represents a higher form of revelation than Jewish Scripture. The texts from both religions were written by human beings with their own challenges, problems that include numerous contradictions and

7. For a more detailed discussion of these problems see Herrick, *Moving Beyond Belief*, 1–23.

text variations, and, on a positive note, special stories of inspiration. I will, however, use CE for "common era," which replaces AD, and BCE for "before the common era," a replacement for BC.

Fifty-five years ago I purchased my first Bible, the Jerusalem Bible, for a New Testament course I was taking in college. Our professor chose this Bible because it was written in plain English and because it came with introductions for each book and exploratory notes scattered throughout. The gospel references cited in this book come from the Jerusalem Bible.

Finally, I would love your feedback. For criticism, praise, or questions, email me at rherrick86@gmail.com.

1

Whisper Ethics

BEFORE DEFINING WHISPER ETHICS, we must examine how both God and humans operate in the world.

Humans act in the world as decision makers. We make decisions in terms of how we see the world. As a political science professor, I had occasion to teach John Locke from time to time. Locke argues that humans are born with a self, a personal identity structure, that is a blank slate. I spent hours in meditation trying to disprove this insight. I was looking for my soul, a deep structure within, that connected me to God. I couldn't find it, which led me to conclude that Locke was correct and I was a biological creature through and through.

The human self operates like a master computer program that defines how we see the world. Genetics plays a major role in defining that master program. Fifty percent of human behavior can be explained by genetics.[1]

The human brain is made up of more than ten billion neurons. These cells are organized into circuits, thousands of miles of them. When neurons become active, they fire an electrical current,

1. See Plomin, *Blueprint*.

which travels along dendrites that function as tiny wires. Synapses are spaces along this highway. There are more than ten trillion of them. Neurotransmitters are chemicals that flood these spaces and function as a bridge. These chemicals slow down, speed up, or change the direction of the traveling neurons, which effects how one sees and experiences the world.

High levels of the neurotransmitter serotonin are known to lower aggression, as are low levels of the hormone testosterone. High levels of the neurotransmitter dopamine are linked to positive emotions and an optimistic view of the world. Norepinephrine is a neurotransmitter that rewards circuits in the brain connected to inhibition and avoidance. People with high levels of norepinephrine organize their lives around preventing unpleasant events from happening. People with low levels seek novel and exciting experiences.[2] The level of these neurotransmitters within each human is genetically determined.

Genetic factors produce what we might call the first draft of our book, but the self is not a fixed entity. It is subject to constant change. Our myriad experiences beginning at birth revise the master program that makes up the self. These experiences include lessons learned from parents and teachers; relationships developed between family members, friends, neighbors, and coworkers; trauma in all its forms; and our successes and failures. Our self is constantly changing as a result of new experiences. Our picture of the world is subject to revision and change.

An important structure within the self is the ego. The ego is a personality structure organized around our insecurities, grievances, and demons. It is based on the assumption we need to be defended, that we are separated, isolated, alone to face the world and thus in need of protection. In pursuit of our defense, the ego generates thoughts that tell us to win, to succeed, to compete. Ego-generated thoughts condemn others and look for revenge when the ego perceives we are threatened. Because of such thoughts, we become self-absorbed, obsessed with our own self-centered concerns, which creates a dense smokescreen within the self, making

2. Le Doux, *Synoptic Self.*

it very difficult to see the needs of others and to process messages reflecting off of divine love.

The evolutionary process based on survival of the fittest reinforces the ego's influence over human consciousness. With survival of the organism as a central concern, the brain generates images in the mind organized around survival. These images function as a voice urging us to act in our own self-interest.

But there is another voice pulsating through our awareness that generates very different thoughts. This voice reflects off of the ground of goodness and love which, based on my experience, comes from God. The God that nourishes my life is known in an encounter. My heart fills when I gaze at stars, stare in silence as a fawn nibbles grass alongside her mother, or sit on the bank of a river watching the water flow by. When I witness suffering or reach out to care for another in need, love again floods my awareness. Meditation on gratitude or loving-kindness toward others can produce a deep peace that really does pass all understanding. These experiences often leave me with a sense of something more. An objective account of what I'm experiencing does not fully explain it.

Because this claim of something more is somewhat vague, let me cite one example from my life that may provide greater clarity. Thirty years ago I spent two weeks with my parents while my father was dying. It was an especially difficult time for me because my dad was only sixty-nine. He seemed so young, and I was a long way from being finished with him.

His problem was congestive heart failure, and he was at home with a heart that was having trouble functioning. Two days before he died I was in the living room with my mother talking about the people to call to report my father's failing condition. The calls were my job.

For some reason Dad decided to walk from their bedroom into the living room, dragging a portable oxygen machine behind him. I was amazed he was able to make the trip on his own, and I am in tears today as I type up the experience of watching him make that effort. My mother immediately left the couch where we were sitting, and they met in the middle of the room.

It was their last dance. Dad had come to say goodbye to my mother. He told her how much he loved her, that marrying her was the best decision he had ever made. It really did look like they were dancing, with my mother holding him closely to provide stability while they relived some of the sacred times in their marriage.

I remained transfixed, sitting on the couch. At some point during this final dance, this special couple became encased in light. Love was radiating throughout the room. You could sense it, feel it, almost touch it. My heart was so filled with love it was bursting. My dad, who I loved deeply, was dying, and yet the world looked so beautiful. Reflecting on the experience later, I was convinced I had been in the presence of God. The reality of the experience was so much more than the objective meeting between my mother and father that was taking place in the center of the room.[3]

An important question is where this sense of goodness and love comes from. I find it embedded in every day life, and Martin Buber best explains it.[4] Buber posits that one's heart fills when two people are engaging in a mutually regarding relationship, when we look upon another as that person wants to be seen and our other regarding stance is reciprocated. Buber concludes that while the love encountered in such relationships is experienced within it actually comes from outside in a space Buber labels as "the between."

I have reflected on Buber's thinking on these matters for years. Where does this love and sense of goodness that is such an important part of my life come from? When I am most honest with myself, I again conclude that I am a biological creature through and through. Love is not an inherent part of my being. The sense of more that so often accompanies my encounters with love suggests Buber is correct. The love I find so deeply embedded in life comes from an outside source; and, for lack of a better term, I refer to this pulsating energy of beauty and goodness as God.

There is another important characteristic about love that points to God. Love transcends. It transcends ideology. It reaches

3. For a thorough and thoughtful treatment of God as more, see Frantz, *God You Didn't Know You Could Believe In*.

4. See his pathbreaking book, *I and Thou*.

out to soften human differences pertaining to race, gender, or sexual preference. It survives death. It cannot be cut off by absence or distance. Viktor Frankl even found it as a prisoner in Nazi concentration camps during World War II.[5]

The analysis above is obviously no proof of God's existence, but it does help to make the reality of God believable. Unfortunately, however, my experiences do not provide any help defining what is behind these encounters. The source of this pulsating energy of goodness, beauty, and love will always remain an impenetrable mystery. I have no interest in creating images of what this God might look like. Lao Tzu begins his famous classic of Chinese philosophy making this point:

> The Tao that be told
> Is not the eternal Tao
> The name that can be named
> Is not the eternal Name.
>
> Tao Te Ching—Verse 1

What is important for this book is that the love encountered as we proceed through the exciting journey of life inspires thoughts. Pay attention to the thoughts floating through your awareness when you witness another person suffering. As your heart fills as you gaze upon a newborn baby, what are you thinking? When you read about some act of injustice in a newspaper, how do you feel? What thoughts emerge from your taking on this information?

The thoughts that emerge from the situations described above reflect off of the sense of goodness and love that is woven into the fabric of life, but the specific content of the message is produced by the individual receiving the encounter. As a result, and to repeat some of what has been said above, Whisper Ethics speaks to thoughts that float through our awareness. The origin of an individual's thoughts reflect off of different grounds or bases. To simplify somewhat, self-centered thoughts reflect off of an egocentric base or structure within the self. Other-directed thoughts

5. See his inspirational book, *Man's Search for Meaning*.

reflect off of a ground of goodness and love that is somehow built into the structure of the universe.

A situation arises, and a person makes a decision to respond. That decision is shaped by thoughts that reflect off of different bases. Different voices may be floating simultaneously through an individual's awareness with respect to the situation presenting itself, a voice stemming from the ego as a structure within the self or a voice reflecting off of a structure of goodness and love embedded within the universe.

We cannot call the voice stemming from a sense of goodness and love the voice of God because this sense filters through an individual's self which gives it a distinctive spin. God does not speak directly to human beings. Instead, the goodness and love we sense generates thoughts that work to point us in a direction beyond self-centered concerns. I call these thoughts "whispers" because they are gentle, never demanding, and much quieter than many of the thoughts generated by ego.

An important part of this equation is hearing these whisper thoughts. The still, quiet voice of goodness and love that floats through our awareness can be crowded out by ego-driven noise. As I point out in the discussion of the human self, the ego in its concern for our defense generates thoughts of revenge and thoughts on the need to win at the expense of others. It often creates a sense of identity defined by amassing great wealth. Such thoughts create a mindset that is self-absorbed and obsessed with self-centered concerns, which creates a thick smokescreen, making it very difficult to hear whisper thoughts inspired by divine love.

The best approach I have discovered for dealing with this problem comes from the practice of mindful meditation. Mindful meditation is designed to help the practitioner move beyond egocentric concerns. It provides a simple technique to quiet this self-centered, ego-driven noise.

With regard to my practice, I begin by sitting in a comfortable chair, closing my eyes, and focusing on my breathing. I center my focus on the process of breathing, one breath in and one breath out, as a way to quiet my mind. Once my mind is quiet and I am at peace, I imagine myself sitting in a tree looking down objectively at my life. I examine my insecurities, what motivates me, what causes anger, situations that create anxiety, the people who bother me. This examination is conducted with honesty but without judgment. The goal is to understand what lies behind this darkness and then to reject it as not representative of my best self. Over time I have come to see that these less attractive aspects of my character are part of an invented self that seeks to protect me, but I have learned that I don't need that kind of protection. When you look at your insecurities and demons directly in the face and refuse to identify with them, they lose their power. The smoke lifts. Your focus broadens. You open space within the self which enables you to see the needs of your neighbor more clearly, and the thoughts emanating from the love and goodness pulsating through the universe become louder.

In addition to the problem of ego driven noise, powerful emotions can drown out whisper thoughts. Feelings are millions of years older than rationality-related thought processes with regards to the evolutionary history of the human brain. Because our brain responds first to our emotionally driven desires, we see a world out there that we want to see.[6] Our focus naturally turns to self-centered concerns. Mindful meditation helps a person understand what is driving their emotions, which weakens their hold over one's consciousness and again opens space within the self which allows one to be more receptive to whisper thoughts stemming from the ground of God's goodness and love.

Twenty-five-hundred years ago, the Buddha argued that the purpose of this type of meditation was to clean the windows of perception so that we can see the world differently. With clean windows, we can more easily tune into thoughts inspired by divine love. When grievances, insecurities, thoughts of revenge and the need to compete in zero-sum games are understood and rejected as not part of our best selves, the whisper thoughts that float into our awareness grow louder. With emotions more under control, thoughts stemming from the love embedded in the universe are

6. See Damasio, *Decartes' Error* and Le Doux, *Synoptic Self.*

more easily recognized. As this reference above to the Buddha suggests, this process of generating thoughts that reflect the needs of others is present in all humans.

There is important evidence that thoughts reflecting divine love are being processed, that Whisper Ethics is working to make the world a better place. Steven Pinker has written a book entitled *The Better Angels of Our Nature: Why Violence Has Declined* which helps to illustrate the workings of Whisper Ethics. He provides a volume of statistical evidence to show that over the long period of human history violence in all its forms has declined. We live at a time of unparalleled stability where rape, war, or the fear of being murdered is not a constant worry.

Ancient societies encountered raids and feuds on a daily basis. Genocide was a common practice in warfare where it was only considered wrong if it happened to your village. From the thirteenth to the twentieth century, homicide rates plummeted in Western Europe.[7] That trend also applied to America, although it was less dramatic because of widespread gun ownership.[8] The two most violent centuries in the modern era were the seventeenth, with its religious wars, and the twentieth century, with its two world wars. Even with these two world wars, however, the death rate by violence in the twentieth century was only 3 percent.

These trends coming from the better angels of our nature also include an end to slavery, a marked reduction in domestic violence against women and crime of all types, reduced discrimination against vulnerable minorities, and a host of positive change with regard to other societal problems.[9] While these trends have moved steadily toward greater peace and societal justice, progress has been uneven in different societies and has proceeded in a two-step-forward, one-step-back process. Homicide rates in the United States climbed significantly from 1960 to the 1980s, but since then these rates have declined by half.[10]

7. Pinker, *Better Angels of Our Nature*, 118.
8. Pinker, *Better Angels of Our Nature*, 95–99.
9. Pinker, *Better Angels of Our Nature*, 149–50.
10. Pinker, *Better Angels of Our Nature*, 125–27.

Pinker suggests that we don't watch television because it distorts what is actually happening in the world. He dismisses terrorism as nothing more than media noise. With the exception of 9/11, the number of Americans killed by terrorists on US soil from 1970 to 2007 is 340. Forty thousand Americans are killed in automobile accidents each year.[11] We have spent billions of dollars, fought two wars costing a trillion dollars or more, and scared a lot of people by our response to this threat which has been greatly exaggerated by the media.

Pinker cites four reasons for these positive trends. The first is more effective government which has led to the rule of law replacing the law of the jungle of the ancient past. Increased international trade has made countries economically dependent on each other which has greatly reduced their incentive to fight. Wars no longer make economic sense.[12]

The age of reason that came with the Enlightenment in seventeenth and eighteenth century Europe led to greater impulse control and self-control over human emotions. People became less prone to violence in all its manifestations because their increased ability to reason made the consequences of violence so much more apparent. The part of the brain directed toward rational and logical thinking has grown tremendously throughout human evolutionary history. As was suggested above, war no longer makes rational sense. European publics, in particular, have turned massively against war.[13]

Fourth, and finally, societal values began changing significantly beginning with the seventeenth century. A culture of human dignity has replaced one based on honor and revenge. Perhaps this change is best summarized by the United Nations Universal Declaration on Human Rights (1948) which affirmed the dignity and worth of every human person. The twentieth century has been defined by rights—civil rights, women's rights, LGBTQ rights, and animal rights, to name a few. Women's rights, which have placed

11. Pinker, *Better Angels of Our Nature*, 344–47.

12. Pinker, *Better Angels of Our Nature*, 680–84.

13. Pinker, *Better Angels of Our Nature*, 690–92.

women in leadership positions, have been particularly important because women are less violent than men.[14]

While admitting humans have a moral sense, Pinker sees religion as part of the problem rather than contributing to the solution. He pictures religion as an ideology, much like nationalism, which is a contributing factor to both wars in the modern era as well as the global battle with terrorism.[15]

Pinker needs to be introduced to Whisper Ethics. Whisper Ethics has nothing to do with ideology. It's about the gentle thoughts generated from the ground of God's goodness and love. These thoughts are behind the moral sense Pinker describes. Because God never coerces, it is easy to ignore thoughts reflecting goodness and love that seek to influence human decision-making. The fact that humans are free to decide creates the two-step-forward, one-step-back process Pinker describes. But God is patient. Her kingdom will come. Yes, there are people who claim to hear God's voice and act in self-centered and destructive ways. But God is winning as Pinker's trends so dramatically demonstrate. Over the long span of human history, the gentle voice inspired by God's goodness and love is making the world a better place.

Sadly, critics will jump all over these conclusions. It's too simplistic, they will say. Lots of people hear what they label the voice of God and act accordingly. Soon after President Biden's election, Christian nationalist pastors called on their followers to wage spiritual warfare. Their crusade began in a nondenominational church in Phoenix, Arizona, two weeks after the November 2020 election. God was telling them Trump was his chosen instrument to bring moral government back to the United States and they should do whatever it takes, including the use of violence if necessary, to achieve God's will. This rhetoric played a prominent role in the January 6, 2021, attack on the United States Capitol.[16]

14. Pinker, *Better Angels of Our Nature*, 692–94.

15. Pinker, *Better Angels of Our Nature*, 676–78.

16. Ward, "Radical Beliefs in Spiritual Warfare."

Life is complex, humans have limits, and thoughts that float through our awareness are often ambiguous. I take inspiration from Jesus and Paul. They both claimed to hear messages reflecting off of divine love; and, in all cases I am aware of, these messages called on them to act in ways that transcended their narrow self-interest. The thoughts stemming from the divine love embedded in the universe called on them to work to achieve economic and social justice, to resolve disputes nonviolently, to be inclusive, and to forgive those who have injured them in some way. Because of our limits as humans, we can never be sure whose voice is floating through our awareness, but when my thoughts match those received by Jesus or Paul, I am confident I am hearing messages inspired by God.

There is one more complication relating to our limits as humans. Hearing the messages from God is one thing. Acting on them can be another matter. Competing voices often present a powerful attraction.

In dealing with the problem, I take inspiration from one of my favorite books, *A Beautiful Mind* by Sylvia Nasar. You may have read the book or seen the movie. Nasar's book documents the life of John Forbes Nash, Jr., the mathematical genius and inventor of the theory of rational behavior. The fields of economics and game theory were fundamentally changed because of his work. For his work in these fields, he was awarded the Nobel Prize for Economics in 1994.

Sadly, underneath the brilliant surface of his life, chaos reined. Nash was diagnosed with paranoid schizophrenia at age thirty. According to Nash, there were two voices in his head, both equally valid: the voice of reason and the voice of aliens.[17]

The voice of aliens produced persistent, scary, debilitating delusions. At one point he saw men at MIT running around in red neckties signaling him. He came to see himself as a religious prophet of great importance with an alternating sense of megalomania and impotence. This voice was extremely disturbing,

17. Nasar, *Beautiful Mind*, 16.

creating within him a sense of apathy, persecution, and social isolation.[18]

To cope with the problem, he tried psychotherapy. He was hospitalized six times, often involuntarily. He received all sorts of drug treatments, shock therapy, and insulin coma therapy where he was placed in an insulin-induced coma. Nash described this last treatment as torture.

None of these therapeutic approaches worked.[19] The voice of aliens was sometimes temporarily reduced, but it kept coming back. This horrible disease ruined his career and marriage.

But there is a happy ending to the story. In 1970, Alicia, his divorced wife, took him back. Because stress often triggers schizophrenic attacks, she offered him a normal life in the academic community of Princeton University, which was relatively stress-free.[20] Nash did the rest. Over the years he had come to understand the processes of the disease, which enabled him to recognize the voice of aliens and to reject it. He decided not to listen to this disturbing voice in his head. It was a constant policing operation.[21] His mind was beautiful because he was able to will his own recovery without help from drugs or therapy.

I love this book because Nash's story is my story. I too am a prisoner of two voices in my head—a voice of love and goodness and a voice of ego focused self-centeredness. My goal in life has been to live the teachings of Jesus in the Sermon on the Mount. The problem is my ego-generated voice has often gotten in the way.

There is, however, a nice ending to my story too. Like Nash, through a constant focus on the problem, I have come to recognize and understand how ego operates in my life. Inspired by the great mathematician, I'm learning to ignore and reject it. Nash's example tells us the mind is a powerful tool for focusing awareness and that humans are decision makers with some control over their fate. The process for me is a constant policing operation that I

18. Nasar, *Beautiful Mind*, 16–17.

19. Nasar, *Beautiful Mind*, 288–313.

20. Nasar, *Beautiful Mind*, 379–88.

21. Nasar, *Beautiful Mind*, 349–57.

sometimes don't win. When the voice of ego is quieted, the voice of love grows louder and comes to dominate more of my awareness. Acts of kindness naturally follow. Whisper Ethics is about hearing the thoughts reflecting off of divine love and acting on them.

I would like to end this chapter by looking at three examples of the workings of Whisper Ethics in action. The first is Jesus' famous parable of the Good Samaritan (Luke 10:30–36). A man on a trip from Jerusalem to Jericho was accosted by bandits and left on the side of the road half-dead. A priest and a Levite representing the religious establishment centered around the temple saw the man suffering on the side of the road and passed him by. Sadly, they practiced a religion based on ritual and belief, an ideological approach that worked to choke out messages generated from divine love.

In contrast, a Samaritan, from a group of people hated by Palestinian Jews, was moved by compassion. He took care of the man, bandaging his wounds and putting him up at an inn so he could recover. Unburdened by ideological belief, this man was able to respond to thoughts reflecting off of the goodness and love embedded within the universe. These thoughts directed him to serve his neighbor in his time of need. The Samaritan then acted on them.

The parable of the sheep and the goats makes the same point (see Matthew 25:31–46). A king at the end of time welcomes sheep into his kingdom. Why? Because, the king answers, when you saw someone who was hungry, you fed them; when thirsty, you gave them drink; when naked, you clothed them. It was another story for the goats. They were cursed and made to enter the fire. Why? Because they ignored those with needs. The key to religion this parable discloses is about hearing the whispering thoughts inspired by God's love and acting on them.

The politics practiced by Abraham Lincoln also illustrate the central themes developed in this book.[22] Abraham Lincoln was not a Christian by most people's definition. While being raised in a small fundamentalist church, Lincoln rejected the Christianity of

22. The historical data regarding Lincoln's life was taken from Meacham, *And There Was Light.*

his parents. He questioned the Bible as the literal word of God, the miracle stories as historically valid, and the belief in Jesus as a divine being. He never became a member of a church. On the other hand, he had a deep sense of a divine presence guiding his life.

Lincoln's life was a testimony to the workings of Whisper Ethics. The bundle of experiences within his self was a mixed blessing. He was raised by anti-slavery parents in Kentucky and Indiana. With them as a child, he attended small Baptist churches that were anti-slavery.[23] In addition, over the course of his life, Lincoln had several encounters with slavery which led to thoughts urging compassion. As a child, he lived along the Louisville-to-Nashville Cumberland Road upon which the slave trade traveled. It was highly likely that he witnessed slaves being herded in chains along this road as a child. He often spoke of a river trip he took in 1841 where he witnessed ten to twelve slaves on a barge in shackles. The sight continually tormented him, almost certainly generating thoughts that slavery was an abomination in the eyes of God.[24]

Because of such encounters, Lincoln came to believe in the existence of a transcendent moral order communicated to humans via conscience.[25] He believed he was acting in accordance with thoughts inspired by God telling him slavery was a moral abomination. This opposition was nonnegotiable because the direction came from God. He remained steadfast in his opposition to slavery despite intense pressure to compromise with the South in order to end a war that was producing horrific casualties on both sides.[26]

On the other hand, Lincoln's self was damaged by insecurities stemming from his birth. He wasn't absolutely sure who his father was. He also grew up in a small, dirt floor cabin in rural Kentucky with no formal education. His elusive sense of identity and embarrassment over his impoverished childhood caused him to doubt his place in the world.[27] This deep insecurity created within Lin-

23. Meacham, *And There Was Light*, 52–55.

24. Meacham, *And There Was Light*, 47–48, 114.

25. Meacham, *And There Was Light*, 194–200, 541.

26. Meacham, *And There Was Light*, 451, 458–62, 467–68.

27. Meacham, *And There Was Light*, 78.

coln a tremendous drive to prove himself which was played out in the political arena. This drive to succeed functioned to diminish the voice of goodness and love within. Lincoln the politician with deep insecurities about his place in the world could also act in ways that diluted God's messages of goodness and love. He refused to get too far ahead of public opinion on the issue of slavery. The American public was deeply racist even in Northern states. As a result, he advocated gradual emancipation throughout most of his career with compensation paid to Southern slaveholders. Once freed, the former slaves were to be sent abroad to live in colonies. He believed that a multiracial democracy based on true equality between races was not possible in America.[28]

Abraham Lincoln was a great man, a highly successful political leader, and a human being. Part of Lincoln's greatness was that he had a deep sense of his limits as a human being. Lincoln the political realist often conflicted with the man who believed it was his duty to implement God's vision of goodness and love in the affairs of the nation. He sensed this conflict and was often uncertain about whose will he was acting upon.

Lincoln's example presents a good case study of how Whisper Ethics works. On many occasions whisper thoughts regarding the grave injustice of holding human beings as slaves floated through Lincoln's awareness. He then acted based on these thoughts and did something about it. Hearing whisper thoughts and acting on them defines Whisper Ethics.

From the perspective of the twenty-first century, many of his preferred solutions to the problem of slavery do not seem to be very enlightened. However, it is important to remember the messages Lincoln received did not come directly from God. He processed the whisper thoughts he received through a self riddled with insecurities and within the climate of opinion (historical context) of mid-nineteenth-century America. And yet no one can deny that important progress was made. To paraphrase the famous statement of Martin Luther King, Jr., Lincoln bent the arc of the moral universe forward toward justice.

28. Meacham, *And There Was Light*, 174–76, 212–13.

2

Applications

THIS CHAPTER ILLUSTRATES THE model developed in the last chapter. Remember, the model claims that whisper thoughts reflecting God's goodness and love embedded within the structure of the universe float through the awareness of specific individuals. As a result, the applications that follow relate to my life experiences. I present them in the hope you will recognize similar situations in your life; and, in addition, gain a clearer understanding of the workings of Whisper Ethics.

UNDERSTANDING THE CONTENT OF WHISPER THOUGHTS: THE PUBLIC SCHOOL DISGRACE

From ages two to ten I lived in Toronto, Canada. While my parents were very happy there with many good friends, they knew their stay would not be permanent. As a result, my mom wanted me to think positively about America. I remember very vividly her telling me as a young boy that America was the only place in the world where people were created equally with an equal opportunity to succeed. She explained that public education was the great leveler that made this possible. Sadly, this belief has become a myth.

While the quality of public schools (K-12) differs greatly among states and even within specific school districts, the overall picture is clear. Most schools in urban settings and many in rural areas receive significantly lower per student funding than their counterparts in wealthier suburban locations. The result is poor facilities (buildings and grounds); lower teacher salaries, leading to a less experienced faculty; larger class sizes; less lab and computer equipment; smaller libraries. These impoverished schools are less likely to have a nurse, a school psychologist, a music or an art teacher. Four- and five-year olds are also far less likely to have preschool opportunities.

In addition to these problems, public schools in America are resegregating at a rapid rate. While significant progress integrating schools was made in the 1970s and 1980s, the Supreme Court changed its tune in 1991 and began chipping away at desegregation enforcement mechanisms. While there are exceptions, few school districts today see desegregated schools as an important priority. White, middle-class parents are opting for private and religious schools as a way to avoid sending their child to a public school with a significant minority population.

This trend has important consequences for impoverished children attending segregated schools. They come to see themselves as inferior, a psychological disposition which weakens their ability to excel in school. Parents who pay private school tuitions often lobby for lower public school budgets in an effort to pay less taxes. The biggest problem, however, is the future of democratic government in America. Democratic institutions will not work well in a multiracial society unless people from different ethnic and religious backgrounds learn about and are comfortable with each other.

The federal government recognized these problems and passed the No Child Left Behind (NCLB) Act in January of 2002. The bill was a collaborative effort of President George W. Bush and Senator Ted Kennedy. The bill led to a significant increase in federal spending for public education. It also gave poor children the right to transfer to better schools, an effort to help them succeed educationally and to reverse the trend toward resegregation of the schools. Federal money was conditional, based on strict accountability, which led to tests, tests, and more tests.

The bill limped to a conclusion six years later with minimal positive results. No money was appropriated to improve buildings or to reduce class size. Many of the funds to improve teaching were never provided. The enforcement mechanisms for student transfers were weak, allowing only 1 percent of eligible students to change schools. Finally, the intense pressure for accountability led to teaching for tests, rote learning, and significant cheating by teachers and principals to show results.

The Obama administration replaced NCLB with Every Student Succeeds, which was passed in the Congress with bipartisan support and signed by the president on December 10, 2015. The bill appropriated 124 billion dollars for the 2016–2020 fiscal years with most funds targeted for poverty schools. The bill was far more flexible on accountability in an attempt to lessen the onerous testing requirements of NCLB.

To no one's surprise, the Trump administration did everything in its power to reduce spending on this program and to weaken the enforcement of it. The Biden administration, as part of its Build Back Better bill, proposed spending 200 billion to make pre-kindergarten free for all youngsters and another 40 billion to provide two years of free community college education for all high school graduates. Unfortunately, Congress was unable to pass the bill.

Often when I read about unjust conditions and policy failures as described above, these are the thoughts that float through my awareness: "This is so unfair." "Politicians opposing help for public schools should be ashamed of themselves." "The American Dream is a myth, a fraud." These thoughts reflect off of the goodness and love whose source is God.

These thoughts would grow louder if you ever visited an urban public school. While I have never undertaken such a trip, Jonathan Kozol has made several. (See his *The Shame of the Nation.*) At one point he takes us into an elementary school in an impoverished section of the Bronx in New York City. As you enter the building, you see several broken windows, cracks in the walls along the hallway, and chipped paint. When you visit a third-grade classroom in a trailer with no air conditioning, there are thirty-five students in the class with one white student, a ten-year old of Russian descent. Your escort into the school explains that the teacher is the third full-time substitute in the last six months. Now imagine you are approached by a little black girl with two missing front teeth. The girl smiles at you and in a soft, shy voice welcomes you to the class.

I know for a fact my heart would melt with compassion. The experience would haunt me for days with thoughts of the huge injustice being perpetrated on these innocent children. The source of these thoughts of injustice does not come from the bundle of experiences that make up my self but rather the underlying source of these thoughts of grave injustice come from God. The point for people who want to become followers of Jesus is to pay attention to these thoughts and to act on them.

WHY I SUPPORT THE WAR IN UKRAINE

The date as I write this section of the chapter is February 24, 2023, the one-year anniversary of Russia's brutal invasion of Ukraine. The Russians came with missiles, tanks and infantry soldiers with the goal of quickly toppling Ukraine's democratically elected government. When Putin's attack stalled and he failed to achieve his initial objective, he launched a barrage of bombing attacks against apartment buildings, hospitals, and schools.

The invasion has led to enormous battlefield casualties on both sides. The bombing against civilian targets has killed thousands of Ukrainian men, women, and children, uprooted 13 million people, and destroyed more than half of the energy grid. In invading Ukraine, Russia has violated the principles of the United Nations Charter that prohibit seizing land by force, wars of aggression, and the targeting of civilians. War crimes have been committed by the Russians in several places throughout the country. Putin was indicted on March 17, 2023, by the International Criminal Court for illegally deporting Ukrainian children to Russia.

The war presents a dilemma for Christians. Support for innocent victims resulting from the Russian invasion is a no brainer. They are our neighbors. But what about the Ukrainian military effort? To support that effort only feeds the violence.

The teachings of Jesus in the New Testament are quite clear. He strongly opposed the use of violence in first-century Palestine. This tradition of Christian pacifism has seen considerable support over the two thousand years of Christian history. Stanley Hauerwas argues that the church is separate from the state.[1] The duty of a Christian is not to solve the problems of the world but to live the teachings of Jesus. The use of violence opposes God's love even when good things can come from it. The church must remain separate from society so that it can fulfill its primary role as being a witness for Christ. The arguments of Hauerwas speak against sending weapons to Ukraine.

Christian realism takes a different position. It argues that pacifism ignores the evil in the world, an evil from which neighbors often need protection. It is deeply concerned with the reality of human sin and the fact that the power of love becomes diluted in large groups. It looks at the world as it is and asks how we can use our power to achieve greater peace and justice. The most famous proponent of Christian realism is Reinhold Niebuhr, who would most likely have been a supporter of sending weapons to Ukraine.

The arguments from both camps make sense to me, but I don't join in the debate. Instead, I listen to the voice inside my head urging me to act in ways that support love and justice. In March of 2003, when the United States invaded Iraq, the first thoughts that came into my head were "so many innocent people will die. We can't do this again." In February of 2022 when Russia invaded Ukraine, my first thought was "Putin is evil. We must do all we can to defeat him."

When thinking about Whisper Ethics, context plays a major role. God does not make universal commands, although many

1. See his important book, *The Peaceable Kingdom*.

conservative Christians believe that is exactly what God does. They want a moral system that is unambiguous. Their favorite source of commands from God is the Ten Commandments. They use the sixth commandment, "You shall not kill," (Exod 20: 13) to justify their pro-life position in the abortion debate.

What these Christians ignore is chapter 34 in Exodus. As you will recall, Moses is away for a long time on the mountain where he receives the Ten Commandments. During that period, the people of Israel construct a golden calf as an aid to worship. When Moses returns and sees the calf, an idol forbidden by the second commandment, he explodes with anger, throwing the tablets which contain the Ten Commandments at the calf which destroys both the calf and the tablets. God is angry too and wants to end his relationship with the people of Israel. (Exod 32: 1–24)

Over time both God and Moses calm down, and God invites Moses back to the mountain to receive new tablets. In chapter 34 of Exodus, God promises to inscribe the exact same ten laws onto new tablets and then for some reason changes his mind. God ends up giving Moses ten different laws as his Ten Commandments. I can just imagine conservative Christians dismissing these new laws as unimportant when compared to the original ten, but that is not the case. The new laws are about how God is to be worshipped, a very important consideration for ancient Jews. Most Old Testament scholars argue that both sets of commandments are human creations, not divine commands.

By contrast, Whisper Ethics is about listening within for the most loving response to a specific situation, but it can be misleading and needs to be approached with humility. Competing voices within the individual's awareness can drown out thoughts reflecting God's goodness and love. Whisper thoughts also come to limited human beings who may not interpret them correctly. Finally, these thoughts come in a whisper because God seems to want to protect human freedom to make independent decisions. As a result, the sense of goodness and love comes without content. This sense filters through an individual's awareness made up of their unique experiences and perspectives. As a result, humans add their own content to the sense of goodness and love from God.

The idea of different experiences and perspectives is an important one. Each person is made up of a unique base outlook created from the psychological structure called the self. This outlook comes from parental instruction, genetic inheritance, core adult experiences, and a variety of other experiences. As a result, the sensations of goodness and love from God can be translated differently for each individual on the receiving end of whisper thoughts. Every time I hear of a new Russian atrocity I see Ukrainians as neighbors who are in need of military assistance in order to defend themselves. Other Christians may be deeply saddened by all the violence and think a better approach would be for the Ukrainians to surrender to the Russians and to resist nonviolently by refusing to cooperate with the puppet government the Russians install.

Because of these limitations, one must be careful never to proclaim that God is commanding such and such a response. The human condition prevents such clarity. The love and goodness of God acts as a backdrop for the thoughts that float through our awareness. This sense of goodness and love is processed through individual selves that differ in terms of the clarity of their perception. Some have denser clouds from ego-related grievances that have remained unexamined. These clouds serve to dilute or block whisper thoughts. As a result, we never hear an actual voice from God. The thoughts that float through our awareness may reflect the sense of goodness and love that is part of the created universe, but the actual content of each thought is a product of human processing.

FINDING WHISPERS FROM GOD IN THE ABORTION DEBATE

On June 24, 2022, the United States Supreme Court in Dobbs v. Jackson announced its landmark decision overturning Roe v. Wade (1973). The Dobbs decision made clear that the United States Constitution does not confer the right of a pregnant woman to have an abortion. The decision granted the right to individual states to regulate abortion in their respective jurisdictions. Finding the right answer to the agonizing question of when to allow for a legal abortion has done more to divide Christians than any other political issue.

The place to begin is to admit a hard truth for many Christians: the Bible will not tell you so. The Christian scriptures have nothing to say about abortion. Despite this significant omission, liberal and conservative Christian writers select different biblical passages to lend support to their preferred positions in an attempt to create the impression that God is on their side. Unfortunately, the arguments in both cases fall short because that is not how God works when it comes to issues like abortion.

With regard to the abortion debate, I had an experience forty-five years ago that changed my life. When I witnessed the birth of our second child, goodness, beauty, and love spread throughout that hospital delivery room. I was awestruck, deeply humbled, and so much in love with my wife and our new daughter. The experience changed the way I looked out at the world. Watching my beautiful wife hold our precious new daughter did me in. The whisper thoughts contained within that experience were both simple and powerful: life is sacred. The idea of aborting that fetus would have been repugnant to me.

Bill Clinton once said that abortion should be legal, safe, and rare. I agree with him. Let's look at the safe part of the formula and create an imaginary scenario. With Roe v. Wade overturned, many states have already passed very restrictive laws outlawing abortion. Imagine a terrified teenager who becomes pregnant, lives in a state where abortions are prohibited, and, in desperation, has an abortion from an unqualified provider. The teenager dies as a result. Because she is the daughter of a close friend, I attend her funeral. What is my heart telling me now? I can imagine receiving very different whispers from the God who was with me when my daughter was born. Context makes a huge difference in the making of ethical decisions.

Let me create one more imaginary example in an attempt to answer a difficult question. How do we hear whispers reflecting divine love when the message goes against deeply held values? How do whisper thoughts speak to a pro-life Christian about abortion? That Christian will most likely not hear whisper thoughts in a sermon, in a Bible study class, or at a pro-life rally. God does not make public pronouncements on political issues. Instead, God-inspired whisper thoughts come to a specific individual who can then apply the thoughts to deciding a political issue if he or she so chooses.

Here's the situation. A fourteen-year-old girl is raped in the backseat of a car. The girl is deeply traumatized and embarrassed by the experience, which makes her unable to report the assault to her evangelical Christian parents. Her fear and dread increase as she misses her period and begins to experience persistent bouts of nausea. In desperation, she eventually confides in her parents.

Any parent with a healthy heart would reach out to their daughter under those circumstances with deep compassion and concern for her future well-being. Ideology breaks down when one's heart is overflowing with a sense of God's goodness and love. Such an encounter causes you to direct your focus on what is good for the other and not on what is important for yourself. Under such conditions, some loving Christian parents might consider allowing their child to have an abortion if they thought it would be in her best interest. In such a case, God's love would have triumphed over ideological belief.

God communicates to humans through a pulsating energy of goodness and love. This energy generates no specific instructions, which leads to the possibility that different individuals will interpret the experience in different ways. Each person gives these underlying sensations of goodness and love content. There are no black and white answers from God to complex human dilemmas like abortion. As a result, it is best for government to remain on the sidelines and allow those directly involved to make the very difficult decisions regarding what is the most loving response for the specific situation they are dealing with.

FORTRESS AMERICA

One of the lessons I remember from my study of US history in high school is that the United States is protected by two oceans on our east and west coasts. Europe's problems could not negatively impact our nation in the early years of its existence because we were separated from Europe by three thousand miles of ocean. Our northern and southern borders were secure because we had friendly neighbors. These conditions continue today.

Our land is rich in natural resources. Our universities are the best in the world. The dollar has been the world's reserve currency for the last seventy-five years, and English is the lingua franca for the global system. We are truly blessed.

More pertinent to the image of fortress, our military is without equal. We spend more than twice our nearest competitor, which is China—$801 billion in 2021 to $293 billion for China. The US spends as much on its military as the next eight countries on the list of the top ten military spenders combined. It's also important to note that ten of the top fifteen spenders are our allies.[2] These allies include thirty-one European states within NATO and several additional allies from Asia. We have more than six hundred military bases in seventy countries, the Pentagon estimates,[3] with some estimates as high as eight hundred. It's interesting to note the ambiguity here. The truth is the US has so many foreign military bases it's hard for the Defense Department to keep track of them all.

How do our competitors stack up? China has a lone ally in North Korea and two overseas military bases in Djibouti and Tajikistan. With the exception of North Korea, China has no friends in Asia. She is surrounded by anxious neighbors which include Japan, Vietnam, South Korea, Indonesia, and India.

Russia has eight foreign military bases, all of which are located in countries that were part of the old Soviet Union before

2. Tian, et al., "Trends in World Military Expenditure."

3. Vines, "Pentagon's New Generation of Secret Military Bases."

1991, with the exception of Syria.[4] Russia faces a European Union with a combined population of five hundred million people and a GDP of $17 trillion. Russia counters with a population of 144 million and a GDP of $1.6 trillion. Taken together the factors described above add up to the American fortress. With the exception of Russian long-range nuclear missiles, no other threats exist to the American homeland. No other country in world history has been as protected.

The sad fact of our huge military dominance is that we have often deployed it. The Congressional Research Service has estimated that the United States has deployed military force overseas more than two hundred times since the end of the Cold War.[5] For all of our good intentions, and this characterization of our actions overseas may be far too charitable, most of these interventions have created outcomes that are disappointing at best. These interventions have led to untold casualties, both military and civilian, have cost trillions of dollars, and have destabilized the states we set out to help.

From the picture above of US military might, several conclusions regarding Whisper Ethics present themselves. First, the image of an American fortress needs to sink in. As I stated above, with the exception of Russian long-range missiles, no other threat exists to the American homeland. Because of this lack of threat, we have little to fear. As fear recedes, we become more open to whisper thoughts as they relate to international affairs.

Second, the less than flattering history of America playing global traffic cop demonstrates that this assumed role has not worked out well. Two different thoughts float through my awareness when I think of these failures. First, let the United Nations do it. We need to build up and reform the UN so that it can take on such a responsibility. Second, I think of the trillions of dollars spent on these military interventions. Imagine if this money had been spent to educate children, build hospitals, dig wells, electrify

4. Wikipedia, "List of Countries with Overseas Military Bases."

5. Torreon and Plagakis, "Instances of Use of United States Armed Forces Abroad, 1978–2022," pp. 14–50.

rural villages, and build roads and bridges. We would be helping to create a new world order. I am convinced these thoughts floating through my awareness come from the structure of God's goodness and love embedded within the universe. You may be having similar thoughts as you reflect on the money squandered on US military operations abroad.

Many Christians are reluctant to become involved in matters of national security and foreign policy. They feel they do not possess the training to intelligently participate in debates on these issues. What they forget is that when they read about the lives lost and the money spent in Afghanistan and think "why couldn't we have spent that money feeding the hungry throughout the world?" that thought reflects the goodness and love of God. Becoming a co-creator with God in making the world a better place is an opportunity we should not pass up. Because it is God who is behind the thoughts urging us to act, we need not worry about our lack of expertise on a specific issue.

CHRISTIAN INTERNATIONALISM: A TWENTY-FIVE PERCENT PLAN

The author of Matthew had Jesus instruct his disciples to make disciples of all the nations (Matt 28:19). This message from Jesus was obviously taken seriously. There are more than two billion Christians in the world today. Maybe it's time for us to act like disciples and do something to honor the prince of peace. I propose that two billion of us stand up and demand our governments reduce defense spending by 25 percent. This money would then be used to fund climate change remediation efforts and economic development for the less developed countries in the world.

The latest figures on world military spending indicate it now exceeds two trillion dollars annually.[6] These disgusting numbers come at a time when military power has become a less useful tool for advancing a country's national interests. Recent United States

6. "World Military Spending Passes $2 Trillion for First Time."

military operations in Iraq and Afghanistan have led to policy failures which have been accompanied by large numbers of civilian and military casualties as well as trillions of dollars spent. The Russians are learning a similar lesson in Ukraine. The health of one's economy has become a much more important indicator of national well-being than armed military power. Economic health increases as military expenditures decline.

American Christians are in the best position to provide leadership on this issue because, as the previous essay suggests, we live in a well-protected fortress. Our military expenditures are so huge that no other country is able to threaten our security. Imagine the effect of an annual expenditure of $500 billion invested in climate change remediation and economic development for less developed countries. We would be working with God to make the world a better place.

You say this sounds like a nice idea, but it is wildly impractical. The countries of the world would never agree to such a plan. I say let's ask God. Please take ten minutes, find a comfortable chair, close your eyes, and focus on breathing—one breath in and another breath out. Once your mind is quiet and at peace, think about this plan and pay attention to the thoughts that float through your awareness. My thoughts are telling me "let's do it. Let's start a movement to honor the wonderful man who two thousand years ago called on his followers to reconcile with their enemies and to seek peace." These thoughts floating through my awareness come from the structure of God's love that is embedded in the universe.

BLACK LIVES MATTER

When I look back on the fifty plus years of my adult life, I see a great deal of progress with regard to civil rights. The neighborhood where I have spent most of my life has been successfully integrated. The tennis club I grew up in now has black members. You can't watch television without noticing black faces in sports, the entertainment industry, and journalism. I have black friends who have had great success in business and the professions.

Sadly, as soon as I start thinking that way, I hear of another police shooting of an unarmed black man. The headlines in newspapers make clear there are serious problems in the criminal justice system. Every part of the system is more harmful to people of color and those without money than it is for white Americans. Legislatures in red states continue to pass laws to restrict the voting rights of people of color.

I have a friend who works for the Stacey Abrams Foundation in Atlanta which is committed to increasing voting turnout for minorities. One night at a party I asked her to explain the problem. In response, she told me the story of a retired African American elementary school teacher who has voted for years at a precinct a ten-minute walk from her home. Recently new laws have closed that precinct, and she now has to take a forty-five minute bus ride to a precinct on the other side of Atlanta. The wait time is often four or five hours.

I recently read an article in the Motley Fool that cited statistics regarding the median net worth of Americans by race. The statistics came from a study conducted by the Federal Reserve. In 2019, the median net worth of white Americans was $189,000, for Hispanic Americans $36,050, and for African Americans $24,000.[7] On June 29, 2023, the Supreme Court ended affirmative action in college admissions. Race can no longer be considered as a factor in admissions.[8] In making that decision, the Supreme Court made it far more difficult for people of color to narrow the glaring income gap cited above.

Reflect on the injustices described above and pay attention to the thoughts that float through your awareness. Those thoughts reflect the love and goodness that come from God. Every time I hear that another black man has been shot I think of Jesus' table. Everyone was invited to eat with him. Inclusion was one of his most deeply held values. Whisper thoughts keep messaging me that much more needs to be done to make black and brown lives really matter so that real inclusion in American society is finally achieved.

7. Caporal, "Average Net Worth."

8. Students for Fair Admissions, Inc. v. University of North Carolina.

THE CYNICAL USE OF FEAR IN POLICY CREATION

In the section on Fortress America, we came to the conclusion that Americans have little to fear from foreign threats to the homeland. The flip side of this conclusion is to ask the question of why such a fortress was created in the first place. The answer is quite simple. Fortress America was created in large part because national security and foreign policy elites exaggerated the threats posed by outside forces. In selling their policies to mass publics, these elites cynically used fear to generate support for their policies. Similarly, in the domestic realm, Republican leaders have used fear to exacerbate the problem of illegal immigration in this country. We'll begin with the problem from a foreign policy perspective.

Ever since the onset of the Cold War during the Truman administration, national politicians and foreign policy elites have used fear in a cynical way to justify bloated defense budgets and the fighting of wars that have had no real connection to our national security. In the early 1950s through much of the 1960s, Soviet communism was described as a global movement directed from Moscow whose goal was world domination. The power of the Soviet military to achieve that goal was greatly exaggerated. Presidential challengers ran on platforms charging "missile gaps," and young children prepared for nuclear war by undertaking drills in their elementary school classrooms. I was one of those children.

This characterization of the communist movement was rarely challenged, which led to two significant miscalculations. The first was that the role of nationalism within the communist world was ignored. Differing national interests led to the Sino/Soviet split. No longer was world communism a unified global threat, but there were in fact two competing centers, and the rivalry was bitter. The second miscalculation was the fact that, after consolidating her empire in Eastern Europe, the Soviet Union operated in the world as a status quo power. Although it may have spoken with a revolutionary tongue, it acted very cautiously. Its goal was to preserve its empire, not to extend it.

One result of these miscalculations was the Vietnam War. Political leaders in the Kennedy, Johnson, and Nixon administrations argued that unless communism was defeated in Vietnam, the nations of Southeast Asia would fall like dominoes eventually threatening the United States. Although we lost the war, only two dominoes fell—Laos and Cambodia. It's a sad irony that these two countries fell not as a response to an out-of-control Communist Vietnam backed by the Soviet Union intent on world domination but rather because the Vietnam War so destabilized the indigenous governments that a small group of highly disciplined leftists was able to seize control in each of the two countries. In the process of fighting the war, thousands of lives were lost and billions of dollars squandered. The hard, cynical truth about this war is that both Presidents Johnson and Nixon admitted in private that the war was not winnable and that a communist Vietnam would not threaten American security.[9]

Later on in the Cold War, the Reagan administration created a similar atmosphere of exaggerated fear of the Soviet Union to justify a huge military buildup. Reagan campaigned on the slogan that the United States military was second to one. He described the Soviet Union as an evil empire that was out to crush us. Between 1980 and 1985, defense spending more than doubled from $142.6 billion to $286.8 billion. The Navy increased its force from 479 combat ships to 525, the Army added soldiers and thousands of Abrams tanks, hundreds of attack fighter jets went to the Navy and Air Force fleets, and the three legs of the nuclear triad—land-based, submarine, and Air Force-launched nuclear missiles—were modernized.[10] All this took place as the Soviet Union was decomposing from within. As the current war in Ukraine conclusively proves, the Russian military continues to have significant problems and is not the global terror it has been painted to be for many years.

The 9/11 attack provided the George W. Bush administration with a golden opportunity to accomplish all of their national security goals. The President described the attack of a small group

9. See Scheer, *Pornography of Power*.

10. Bowman, "Reagan Guided Huge Buildup in Arms Race."

of stateless terrorists as placing the survival of the nation at stake. Secretary of Defense Rumsfeld characterized the world after the attack as a very dangerous place. There was a steady drumbeat of fearmongering from administration officials and congressional hawks which turned the Global War on Terror into a crusade that made dissenting views difficult to express.

This atmosphere of fear allowed the Bush administration to double the regular defense budget during the eight years it was in office. High-tech weapons were added to all four branches of the military which had nothing to do with fighting terrorists. Senator Joseph Lieberman of Connecticut got the Pentagon to order thirty new attack submarines at a cost of seventy-five billion dollars which the Pentagon didn't want. It just so happened that the submarines were made in Lieberman's state. In a speech on the Senate floor, Senator Lieberman made the case for these subs in terms of dealing with the terrorist threat. Nobody questioned this silly assumption.[11]

The Bush administration also used fear to sell the Iraq War. Administration spokesmen painted Saddam Hussein as a Hitler with a fearsome military that included weapons of mass destruction. This "awesome" military machine had been decisively defeated in 1991 by the United States in Desert Storm in six weeks, but no one was expressing this contradiction. The Bush administration never informed the public that both the CIA and the UN weapons inspection team had grave doubts about Iraq's possessing nuclear weapons. As with Vietnam, the war was fought with disastrous consequences—thousands of civilians and soldiers killed, massive social and economic disruption, and a two-trillion-dollar price tag.

Moving to domestic politics and the immigration problem, for Republicans it's all about the "great replacement," a conspiracy theory that there is a coordinated, active, and covert effort on the part of Democrats to replace the white majority. Former Fox News host Tucker Carlson claimed on his show in July 2022 that the "great replacement" was no conspiracy theory but the key to the

11. Sheer, *Pornography of Power.*

Democrat party's electoral strategy. According to Carlson, Democrats want wide open borders and speedy amnesty so illegals can vote. The Democrats have orchestrated an invasion at the border.[12]

Republicans played the immigration card in the recent 2022 midterm elections. America's Voice documented three hundred campaign ads featuring the invasion theme in 2022. Four thousand ads focused on immigration in general.[13] No one disputes the fact that the current immigration system is under stress. It was not built to handle the current level of migratory flows that confront it. Rather than search for compromise solutions to the problem, Republicans have weaponized the issue. They repeatedly claim without evidence that illegal immigration is tied to voter fraud and crime. Their solution is to build walls and deport those who are here illegally. Their goal with the issue is to inflame their base whose members are paranoid about the white race losing their majority status in the country.

What happens when fear colors politics? Military empires are built, and the political system is unable to construct a comprehensive solution to the immigration mess. Whisper thoughts reflecting the God of love and goodness cannot be heard. When you're afraid or angry, the loudest voice in the room carries the day. That voice often reflects grievances, conspiracy theories, revenge, and otherwise simplistic solutions to a problem. In such an environment, whisper thoughts become harder and harder to hear.

THE POLITICS OF GLOBAL WARMING

There are two right-to-life issues of critical importance to the future health of the planet. The first is climate change. The place to begin is with the science that explains the issue.

There is a broad consensus among scientists that global warming is occurring because of human activity. The basic science is simple to understand. The burning of fossil fuels has increased

12. Miller and Kieffer, "Hate and Extremism in the Mainstream," 11–13.

13. Miller and Kieffer, "Hate and Extremism in the Mainstream," 11–13.

the level of carbon dioxide in the atmosphere by 40 percent since the beginning of the industrial age. This carbon dioxide acts like a blanket by refusing to allow heat to escape from the atmosphere. The result is global temperature rise. During the twentieth century global surface temperatures have increased by 1.33 degrees Fahrenheit. Computer models suggest that by 2100 the global surface temperature will rise an additional 2.0 degrees F at minimum with a maximum possible gain of 10.2 degrees F.[14] That last figure, if ever reached, signals global catastrophe.

Global warming is causing glaciers to melt, leading sea levels around the world to rise. This increased heat adds moisture to the atmosphere and increases the energy in the climate system which incites extreme weather. Forest fires in places like California and more recently in Quebec have erupted with increased intensity and frequency. Increased levels of carbon dioxide have also found their way into the oceans which changes the chemistry of the water thus posing a significant long-term threat to several species of aquatic life. In addition, a changing climate has destroyed habitat for many of God's creatures, leading to their deaths.

As I put the finishing touches to this book, scary effects continue to emerge. The ocean temperature off the tip of Florida reached 100 degrees Fahrenheit in late July 2023. Even more scary, a recent study warns that Atlantic Ocean currents are in danger of collapsing. As Artic ice melts, the cold water that pulls the current northward is warming which slows the natural processes that move currents. The collapse of that system will disrupt rain patterns in India, South America, and West Africa, which will endanger food supplies for billions of people.[15]

Significant expenditures now to contain this global scourge will pay dividends for the future because out-of-control global warming will have enormous negative economic consequences. The real danger with this issue, however, is that there is no forgiveness. Greenhouse gases emitted today into the atmosphere will remain a problem for a thousand years or more.

14. Lindsey and Dahlman, "Climate Change: Global Temperature."

15. Carrington, "Gulf Stream Could Collapse."

The climate change problem is insidious because it is creeping up on us largely unseen. The effects will be most severe for younger generations. I do not need to hug my granddaughter, however, to know that whisper thoughts are telling me to do something about it, but here is the more important Christian problem as I see it. Most of the people I know believe that climate change is real, but few are doing much about it. They are looking for technological solutions. They seem to be unwilling to change their lifestyle in any meaningful way in an attempt to combat it. To be a follower of Jesus requires we listen to our whisper thoughts and act. These thoughts are messaging me to moderate my way of living. Like all Americans receiving such messages, the time has come to act.

TRY A LITTLE KINDNESS: THE POLITICS OF ENGAGEMENT

I was walking with a good friend a few years ago, and another white supremacist rally was in the news. "Joe, what can we do about these people?" I asked. "How can we change their hate-filled values?"

"We love them," Joe responded. "Engage with them. Stop demonizing them. That was Martin Luther King's approach to such people." I had two immediate thoughts regarding Joe's answer. First, Jesus would have agreed with him. Second, such a strategy reminded me of one of my favorite books, *Brother to a Dragonfly*, by Will D. Campbell. Campbell was born and raised in rural Louisiana. After graduating from Yale Divinity School in 1952, he returned to Louisiana to become a Baptist minister. Two years later he was sent to the University of Mississippi to become the Religion-in-Life Director with instructions to assist in the integration of the school. *Brother to a Dragonfly* begins there. Though it is an autobiographical story with several dimensions, the part I found most intriguing was his civil rights work in the South. After a year or two at Ole Miss, he decided he could make his most lasting contribution by ministering to the Ku Klux Klan. That experience both enriched and changed his life. As my friend Joe suggested, he decided to engage with people who held very different values from his own.

Fifty years ago, while a graduate student at Tulane University, I heard a story that speaks to this issue. The football program recruited a kid from rural Louisiana whose father was a prominent white supremacist. The recruit was reputed to share his father's values. In order to minimize tensions on the team, one of the coaches asked two African American players to befriend the recruit. They did, and it changed the recruit's life. He acquired new friends and very different values.

Engagement works in the real world of international politics too, and we need to try it with Iran. When the Shah of Iran was removed from office in 1979, the United States severed diplomatic relations with Iran, a situation that remains in place today. A revolutionary Iran has been a difficult country to deal with as was seen with the hostage crisis from November 1, 1979 to January 20, 1981 and her "seeming" rush to create nuclear weapons more recently. Harsh rhetoric, economic sanctions, cyber-attacks, and diplomatic isolation were unable to convince Iran to change course with regard to those weapons.

The Obama administration tried a new approach and engaged Iran. With this in mind, they began negotiations on the nuclear weapons issue. This policy change allowed both sides to reach an agreement to stop Iran, at least temporarily, from acquiring nuclear weapons. The deal was signed on July 14, 2015, and there is a universal consensus that Iran has lived up to the terms of the agreement. The deal is not a permanent fix, however. There are several parts to the agreement which expire at different times. Iran will have no incentives to continue with the agreement after those expiration dates unless a different tone develops in our relations which leads to reduced tensions between the two countries and concrete economic gains as a result of these reduced tensions are made by the Iranians.

History tells us that revolutions moderate over time. The generation following a revolution grows tired of ideology and sacrifice and yearns for a more normal existence that centers around a good job and a stable family life. With regard to Iran, the second generation is now middle-aged and exhibiting those characteristics. In addition, Iran has the largest middle class in the Middle East. It has large numbers of women with professional-level educations. Its elections for president, parliament, and at the municipal level have issue significance, pitting reformers against deeply conservative religious ideologues. Though many would disagree, these characteristics make it the most democratic country in the Middle East. Under such conditions a policy of engagement would reap significant benefits.

The strength of the middle class in Iran was both seen and tested in recent riots. These riots and protests broke out on September 16, 2022, in response to the death of twenty-two-year-old Mahsa Amini. Amini had been arrested and brutally beaten by the Guidance Patrol for wearing an improper hijab in violation of Islamic law. The protests that followed were widespread, involving thousands of citizens, and they threatened the revolutionary government in a significant way. The protests lasted well into the new year, demonstrating once again the power and determination of Iran's middle class.[16]

How does one engage another country diplomatically? The first step is to end the harsh rhetoric which often expresses half-truths at best. The second step is to increase trade and investment between the two countries. Over time exchange programs should be encouraged. In the case of Iran, apologizing for our role in organizing the coup that overthrew Prime Minister Mohammed Mosaddeq in 1953 which led to the autocratic rule of the Shah would be electric in its effect. Unfortunately, nation states rarely admit mistakes of that kind.

A policy of engagement, however, does not mean you ignore issues causing tensions between the two countries. With regard to Iran, her support of terrorist groups in Lebanon (Hezbollah) and Yemen (the Houthi rebels) is disturbing. These issues are dealt with quietly, diplomatically, behind closed doors with the hope of steering the country in a different direction over time.

16. "What Happened to Mahsa Zhina Amini?"

Sadly, the Trump administration chose a different course. His administration initiated a policy of massive pressure with the goal of toppling the regime. The campaign included harsh rhetoric, the scrapping of the nuclear weapons agreement, and the assassination of the revered general Qasem Soleimani. The policy change did not succeed in toppling the regime, but it rather propped it up. On June 19, 2021, ultra-conservative judiciary chief Ebrahim Raisi was elected president. Raisi, who replaced the well known moderate Hassan Rouhani, is the most hardline president Iran has seen in decades.[17]

Most foreign policy analysts cringe when they think about the possibility of applying a little kindness to the real world of international politics. However, foreign policy elites are not immune from receiving whisper thoughts. It seems possible President Obama acted in response to such messages when he changed course and engaged Iran in nuclear negotiations. While we can't get into the head of President Carter, so many of his policies seemed to reflect the better angels of his nature. He lived his life in a way that suggested he both heard and acted on thoughts reflecting the love and goodness of God.

MY GAY FRIEND

Gay marriage is an issue of public policy only because conservative Christians believe the Bible to be the inerrant word of God. In point of fact, conservative Christians have it right. In Rom 1:27, Paul forthrightly condemns homosexuality as a sin. What conservative Christians ignore is Rom 13:11–12. In this passage, Paul proclaims the imminent return of Jesus within the first century: "the Day is at hand." Paul was obviously wrong about this important prediction. Maybe he was wrong about homosexuality too. Biblical passage pickers ignore passages that do not support their preconceived positions.

17. CNN Staff, "Trump Dashed Dreams of Reform in Iran."

Whisper Ethics suggests you pay less attention to the Bible and befriend a gay person instead. When my gay friend told me he was going to marry his long-time partner, my heart soared. My thought was, "That's great news. It's about time." Christians who oppose gay marriage practice a religion centered around belief. It's an ideology that doesn't touch their heart. The driving force in ethical decision-making which characterizes Whisper Ethics is the love and goodness of God. You receive thoughts that reflect off of that sense of goodness and love most clearly when you relate to another person without judgment or preconceived opinions about him.

Finding a friend is what the larger LGBTQ issue is all about from a Christian perspective. Many years ago as a graduate student at Tulane I spent a lot of time in the library. So did a Laura who was named Larry at birth. I remember having coffee with her one morning in the third floor of the library where we both worked; and, upon returning to do my own research, I thought that what Laura really wanted was for me to see her as a woman, a thought floating through my awareness, reflecting the structure of love embedded in the fabric of life. Over time that happened, and I give her all the credit for helping me come to that understanding. She was then and I'm sure is now a gem of a person.

In many ways, this issue is all about Martin Buber, my favorite theologian. Buber's philosophy describes what happens when you treat others with love and respect, as a thou (someone special) rather than as an it (an object). When you see a person as a thou and the empathy is returned, your heart fills. Pay attention to the thoughts that float through your awareness when that happens. The last thing to occur to you would be the thought that homosexuality is a sin.

THE NUCLEAR WEAPONS SCOURGE

During the Cold War years, the United States and the Soviet Union built nuclear bombs. By 1986, the U.S. arsenal included 23,000 such bombs with the Soviet arsenal reaching 40,000. Each of these bombs was, at minimum, several times more powerful than the nuclear bomb that destroyed Hiroshima in 1946. The yield of some of the larger bombs was one thousand times more powerful than the ones used at the end of World War II.

These national security policies of the two states were insane, morally bankrupt. An all-out war between the two countries would have ended human life on the planet. And we came so close!

US government officials during the Cold War claimed we needed such an arsenal to deter the Soviet Union. Nuclear deterrence is achieved when a country can survive a nuclear first strike and retaliate with devastating consequences. These claims by government officials were untrue. Nuclear deterrence can be achieved with one Ohio submarine carrying Trident II missiles which provide enough firepower to totally destroy twenty-four Russian cities." Such a submerged submarine is virtually invulnerable to attack. The US has several of such submarines.[18]

The United States nuclear arsenal was designed for war fighting. Our weaponry was organized in such a way as to "decapitate" the Soviet Union with a first strike. Such a strategy meant attacking Soviet command and control centers as well as their missile silos and air bases. In launching the attack, enough weapons were to be held in reserve to threaten Soviet cities if they fought back.

There are three horrible problems with this strategy. First, the Soviets might respond with a launch on warning during a crisis when the arsenals on both sides were on hair-trigger alert. Second, submarine commanders, and those commanding missile sites the US failed to destroy, may calculate that their country was destroyed already and retaliate in anger. The result of these first two problems is general war and the end of human life on the planet.

The third problem assumes we succeed. Such an attack would kill millions of innocent people living in Russia, neighboring Europe, and China from the blasts themselves, from firestorms resulting from the blasts and from radiation fallout. Most of the dead would be innocent civilians. I don't know how any sane person could pull the trigger on such an attack.[19]

18. Wikipedia, "UGM-133 Trident II."

19. For a detailed discussion of these horrible consequences see Ellsberg,

During the Cold War, tactical nuclear weapons designed to be used in battlefield situations were deployed to protect Europe from a Soviet invasion. Very soon after the invasion US policy was to counterattack with tactical nuclear weapons. The reason for the policy was to save money. Deploying sufficient conventional forces to deter an attack was seen as being too expensive. The problem with such an approach is that it placed the lives of millions of innocent Europeans at risk.

Use of nuclear weapons was threatened against North Korea and China in 1953 in an attempt to end the Korean War. A similar threat was made against China in 1958 in the Quemoy and Matsu Crisis, two islands claimed by Taiwan which China threatened to occupy. First use was also threatened against the Soviet Union during the Berlin Crisis in 1961, and by Nixon during the Vietnam war.[20] Putin has played the nuclear weapons card in the current war in Ukraine. The world has been lucky that nobody called our bluff or that of the Russians.

In a fascinating book on the subject entitled *The Doomsday Machine*, Daniel Ellsberg points out another scary problem. The idea that only the president can decide to use nuclear weapons is a myth. Beginning with the Eisenhower administration, theater commanders were given the right to initiate the use of nuclear weapons under certain conditions. This policy was put in place to guarantee deterrence in the event Washington was destroyed and theater commanders were unable to receive a presidential order.[21]

The Soviet Union also had such a policy which came close to producing Armageddon during the Cuban missile crisis in 1962. The Kennedy administration quarantined Cuban waters to prevent further missile-related equipment from the Soviet Union reaching the island. The administration warned the Soviet Union that their four submarines in Cuban waters would have to leave the area. An official explained to Moscow that American destroyers would drop hand grenades into the water to signal the subs to surface.

Doomsday Machine, 134–35.

20. See Ellsberg, *Doomsday Machine*, 53, 146, 169, 290.

21. Ellsberg, *Doomsday Machine*, 282–84.

The four submarines never received that message. Upon hearing the exploding hand grenades, one sub commander believed he was under attack and that the war had started. Because he was unable to communicate with Moscow, he and the other officer holding the nuclear keys wanted to attack with a nuclear armed torpedo to defend the honor of the Soviet Navy. By chance the squadron commander was on board holding a third key, and he refused. That refusal to initiate a nuclear strike most likely saved the world.[22]

Since the end of the Cold War some rationality has returned to this madness. The START 1 treaty, signed by the United States and Russia on July 31, 1991, set a limit of 6,000 nuclear warheads for each side with a limit of 1,600 ICBMs and bombers. The treaty reduced the number of operational strategic warheads by 80 percent. The New START treaty entered into force on February 5, 2011, following Senate ratification. This treaty limits the number of deployed launchers (ICBM, submarine, and bombers) to seven hundred. A total of 1,550 nuclear warheads can be deployed on these launchers. [23]Just recently President Putin announced that Russia was suspending its participation in this last of the nuclear arms control treaties. What happens now is anyone's guess as the last remaining guardrail is dismantled.

Ten weeks after his inauguration, President Obama went to Hradcany Square in Prague and spoke about his deep interest in reducing nuclear weapons. He went so far as to suggest that nuclear weapons states seek a world without such weapons.[24] In making that speech, it seems most likely he was responding to whisper thoughts reflecting divine love that he had been receiving for many years.

Obama was able to succeed in implementing his vision as I indicate above with the signing of the New Strategic Arms

22. For readers interested in the classic study of the Cuban Missile Crisis, see Allison and Zelikow, *Essence of Decision*. A good summary can be found in Ellsberg, *Doomsday Machine*, 179–208.

23. A good summary of U.S./Russian arms control treaties from START 1 in 1991 to NEW START in 2010 can be found in Jentleson, *American Foreign Policy*, 532–36.

24. Pauly, "Remembering the Prague Speech."

Reduction Treaty (New Start) between the United States and Russia in April 2010. Sadly, after this initial achievement, his efforts for further progress on this issue stalled. There are many reasons for the failure of his vision for a nuclear weapons-free world, but there is one that is particularly concerning to me.

Every sane person who is reading this analysis is receiving whisper thoughts that there must be a better way to provide for national security. There is a huge issue of complacency in the spiritual world. Every religious person on the planet is having these thoughts. Why didn't Christians from around the world rally behind Obama's vision and insist that their countries negotiate with him in good faith? We all have a responsibility to work with God to make the world a better place. Becoming a follower of Jesus means more than giving at the collection plate. We must learn how to listen to thoughts derived from divine love and then act. I can guarantee you thoughts of this type are flooding the awareness of all religious people who are not blinded by ideological concern or in possession of selves damaged by fear and toxic grievances. The time has come for Christians to stand up and act.

AMERICA'S UNIQUE PROBLEM WITH GUN VIOLENCE

Right-wing conservatives have reinterpreted the second amendment to the Constitution that relates to gun ownership. If you read the history of debates over this issue during our formative years, it is clear the intention of the authors of the Bill of Rights was to grant members of state militias the right to own guns. This was important because there was no standing national army at the time, and the founding fathers believed citizens needed protection. Read the Second Amendment to the Constitution. Though far from unambiguously stated, the amendment seems framed to pertain to members of state militias.[25]

25. For a brilliant analysis of the grammatical issues pertaining to the Second Amendment, see Bergon, "Guns and Grammar."

Over the last twenty-five years these right-wing conservatives have changed this original meaning to the right of every individual to own a gun. As a result, it is no mystery that death from gun violence has skyrocketed in this country. The number of firearm deaths have climbed in the United States from 37,155 in 1991 to 48,830 in 2021.[26] Sadly, this is a good example of American exceptionalism. We are the only country in the Western world with this problem.

When I think about this issue and its many innocent victims, every fiber of my being screams out that this is wrong. Whisper thoughts are telling me that gun ownership for purposes other than hunting is evil because it places so many innocent people at risk.

Such thoughts reflecting off of divine love are ones many conservative Christians seem to be unable to hear. Whisper thoughts are presenting themselves to them, but their hearts are closed. If the psychological assumptions behind Whisper Ethics are correct, these Christians need to do some inner meditative work to purge the grievances, insecurities, and fear clouding their selves. Sadly, for many of these Christians, their religion is all about correct belief, an ideology that fails to connect with their heart, an ideology that makes it more difficult for them to discern thoughts reflecting the love from God.

A MESSAGE PERTAINING TO CENTRAL AMERICA

In the fall of 1970, I enrolled in a PhD program in Latin American Studies at Tulane University. Early on during my first semester there, I attended a lecture on the causes of political instability in Central America. The professor giving the lecture was a specialist on Guatemala, Honduras, and El Salvador, which were the three countries he focused on. I remember the thrust of that lecture quite clearly, but I must admit to doing a little research on the subject in preparation for writing this short essay.

26. "Mass Shootings in the United States."

It embarrasses me to point out that US government policy over the last two hundred years has played an important role in creating this problem of weak political institutions in these three countries. We have treated Central America as if it was our own backyard. We have intervened countless times in these countries to protect our economic interests, to maintain law and order, to prevent a government we did not like from assuming power, and to place someone in power who would do our bidding. I cannot think of one intervention that was made to support a government championing economic and political reform. Since the end of the Cold War, we have largely ignored these countries.

With regard to Guatemala, Col. Arbenz Guzman won a fair election in 1950 as a social reformer. When he initiated land reforms that threatened the assets of the United Fruit Company, the CIA organized an invasion to overthrow him. This led to a thirty-five-year civil war between US-backed governments and left wing guerillas.[27]

The same pattern applies to Honduras. In the late nineteenth century, the Honduran government granted land and substantial economic incentives to American agricultural and infrastructure companies. American troops were sent to Honduras in 1903, 1907, 1911, 1912, 1919, 1924, and 1925 to protect those interests.[28] Those American companies did a good job sending home profits to American investors but did little to help Honduran political leaders create a diversified economy and stable political institutions.

In the case of El Salvador, political and economic instability ruled from the late nineteenth to the middle of the twentieth century. Coups, revolts, and authoritarian governments backed by the United States dominated this period. The opposing groups within the country fought a devastating civil war which dominated Salvadoran society from 1979 to 1992.[29]

I can remember quite clearly leaving that lecture for the twenty-minute walk home. I decided right then and there on a specialty. I would research and write about United States policy

27. Jentleson, *American Foreign Policy*, 18–22.

28. Smith, *Talons of the Eagle*, 50–52.

29. Smith, *Talons of the Eagles*, 182–83.

toward Central America with the clear intention of creating a more enlightened approach. This message resulted from whisper thoughts reflecting off of God's love and goodness that were floating through my awareness.

LAURINBURG, NC

Our family moved to Laurinburg, North Carolina, in 1978 when I assumed a position on the faculty of the University of North Carolina at Pembroke. Laurinburg is a small town on the South Carolina border between Charlotte and the North Carolina beach. When the town newspaper was delivered that first week we were there, the headline read, "Cotton is Still King."

In other respects, however, it was a surprising first week for a Yankee liberal from Massachusetts. I learned that our eldest daughter had become the campaign manager for a fellow student who was running for president of the school. He was black. Our two younger children went to an elementary school where the principal and several teachers were African American. I was amazed at how smoothly these fully integrated schools functioned.

Five years later, through an interesting set of circumstances, I became chair of the Human Relations Commission for the county. The three races within the county received equal representation—white, black, and Native American. During my five years on the Commission, we successfully established a teen pregnancy council and diffused some tense labor relations issues. The three racial groups worked extremely well together.

During the 1970s and 80s, the economy of the town was thriving. There were five major industrial plants within the county. Unemployment was extremely low, and the average wage was twenty dollars an hour. Crime was something you rarely heard about. Most of the people we knew didn't lock their doors at night.

Four years ago we returned to visit our former next door neighbors who still lived in the town and with whom we have remained in close contact. It was a different place. Four of the five industrial plants had left the area. The unemployment rate was close to 30%, and the average wage had declined to $12.50 an hour. The schools were underfunded, and white parents with money were sending their children to Christian academies. Crime and opioid addiction had become major problems. The three major racial groups were no longer working well together, with a tribal mentality replacing the spirit of cooperation I had encountered thirty years prior to our return visit.

Three years ago I had the privilege of telling this story to Andrew Young, who provided me with an interesting perspective on the problem of systemic racism in this country. I met Ambassador Young at a party given by a close friend to raise money for a predominately African American college in Atlanta. Amazingly, I had half an hour, one-on-one, with the former United Nations ambassador. We talked about his early years with Dr. King, his tenure as mayor of Atlanta, and his years in the Carter administration.

When I told Ambassador Young of my Laurinburg experience, he smiled and said, "You know, Rick, the problem of systemic racism in this country is not all that difficult to understand. As your Laurinburg example tells us, the cause is primarily economic. When white folks have good jobs, they make good neighbors. When they are unemployed and scared or underemployed and resentful, there are problems."

Making progress with the problem of systemic racism in America will involve building-up African Americans with better health care, better education, and an economy that provides them with good jobs. It will also involve major reforms within the criminal justice system, and national legislation to protect minority voting rights.

On the other hand, we must not forget that a major cause of the problem is white resentment and fear. My Laurinburg example suggests that these anxieties among white Americans are legitimate. Twenty-first century capitalism driven by free trade and the digital revolution has decimated rural America, creating large-scale economic inequality and high levels of unemployment. A study conducted by the Rand Corporation from 1975 to 2018 found that $50 trillion has moved from the bottom 90 percent of the population to the top 1% percent.[30] The negative consequences from the revolutionary changes driving our economy will only get worse as captains of industry strive to increase profits with innovative technology and cheap sources of labor.

I worry about this problem all the time with whisper thoughts messaging me in one way or another not to forget the victims. The use of coal must end soon if we are going to save the climate from heating beyond control, but what about coal miners? They are innocent victims. Trucks will soon be driven autonomously. That will save money, but what will we do with all the unemployed truckers? They too are innocent victims. Similar examples exist for all segments of the economy.

To repeat what I said above, whisper thoughts are telling me we must not forget the victims, and these thoughts reflecting divine love contain much wisdom. Democratic government will not survive the chaos resulting from millions of Americans deciding they have no place in the modern digital world that is rapidly coming upon us.

THE MYTH OF AMERICAN EXCEPTIONALISM

American exceptionalism is the belief that the United States is unique in the world and exemplary when compared to other nations. What makes us distinctive are our values, political system, and history. Many take this a step further and claim the United States is morally better than other countries, and as a result, God has given us permission to transform the world in our image.

The idea for American exceptionalism was first entertained by the French historian Alexis de Tocqueville who traveled throughout America in 1831. The idea of our exceptionalism is a major theme in his book, *Democracy in America*, which was published in 1835. American Protestantism nourished the idea with the belief that God had especially blessed the United States of America.

30. Price and Edwards, "Trends in Income From 1975 to 2018."

I am proud to be an American and buy into the myth in part. The American Revolution and our founding documents were clearly unique in the world of the eighteenth century. We were a nation created around ideals rather than ethnicity or a dominant elite group. Abraham Lincoln may have put it best when he said at Gettysburg that America is a nation "conceived in liberty and dedicated to the proposition that all men are created equal."

In order to protect that liberty, the founding fathers created a democratic system based on checks and balances which provide guardrails preventing the government morphing into tyranny. As a political scientist who specialized in comparative government, I studied many foreign political systems. Without question, I can tell you that the political system our founding fathers created is brilliant. It has provided for political stability, protection of individual liberty, free and fair elections, and wealth generation that is unique in the world.

There is another part of that myth, however, that I find terribly disturbing: namely, the idea that the United States is morally better than other countries in the world, which gives us the unique mission to transform other countries in our image. This notion is not supported by our 250-year history, and it has led to dangerous American meddling in the world.

The idea of our moral superiority ignores the history of slavery in this country. Slaves were dehumanized and often grossly mistreated beginning with the colonial period in the eighteenth century and continuing for much of the nineteenth century. Although the slaves were freed after the Civil War, they remained in a condition of de facto servitude because of the failure of Southern states to implement the Fourteenth Amendment to the Constitution which affords equal protection for all American citizens under the law. America never really became serious about African American civil rights until the 1960s.

The idea of moral superiority also ignores the history of our treatment of Native Americans for much of the nineteenth century. Protestant missionaries tried to cram the Bible down their throats which destroyed their beautiful native culture. Worse still, we stole their land and decimated their male braves on the battlefield, forcing the few who survived to live on reservations which often lacked fertile land and adequate natural resources.

We also stole land from Mexico—lots of land. In 1844 James K. Polk ran on a platform of extending U.S. territory in the West to the Pacific Ocean. Soon after assuming office, he went to work to operationalize his dream of manifest destiny. He began by offering to buy the land from Mexico. When the Mexicans refused, he manufactured a crisis and then sent in troops in what became known as the Mexican-American War. (1846–1848) Major General Winfield Scott was quickly able to throw Mexican troops from this land which led to their surrender as American troops marched toward Mexico City. At the treaty of Guadalupe Hidalgo, which was signed in 1848, Mexico ceded California, Nevada, Utah, and parts of Arizona, Colorado, New Mexico, and Wyoming to the victorious Americans.

In the essay on Central America, I gave examples of United States interventions in that part of the world to protect American interests which have been a contributing factor to political instability in several Central American states. Dov H. Levin has written a book entitled *Meddling in the Ballot Box: The Causes and Effects of Partisan Electoral Interventions*. The book documents American interventions throughout the world. From 1946 to 2000, the United States interfered in eighty-one foreign elections. During that same period, the Soviet Union and then Russia after 1991 intervened in a total of thirty-six foreign elections. Levin argues that both countries used such interventions to prevent candidates from winning who they believed would endanger their interests once in office.

Following the end of the Cold War, a group of neoconservative intellectuals began to advocate for an American empire. No one could challenge us now, they argued. America's time to dominate the world stage had come. The purpose of the empire was to fulfill America's mission to bring democratic government and freedom to the world. Military intervention in the affairs of others was seen as a good thing. Neocons, as they were called, like Paul

Wolfowitz, Elliott Abrams, Richard Perle, and Paul Bremer, gained positions in the George W. Bush White House and were able to get the president on board with their agenda. President Bush believed he was on a holy mission in sending thousands of American troops into Afghanistan and Iraq to bring capitalism and democratic government to these two impoverished states torn apart by ethnic conflict. Bush lost his gamble with disastrous consequences for lives lost and trillions of dollars squandered.[31]

Admittedly the history outlined above is one-sided. It only looks at the dark side, and I'm sure a good case can be made documenting some of the enlightened events in our history. But the point is to argue that Americans have no special claim to moral righteousness. We are human beings like everyone else in the world with the capacity for both goodness and evil. To ignore the dark side of our history makes it more likely that similar mistakes will be made.

The history above suggests that trying to impose your values on others invariably leads to negative consequences. This applies to both individual, one-on-one relationships and the relationships between states. I have become better, though not perfect, in solving the first problem through mindful meditation. By cleaning the windows of my perception, I feel less need to impose my values on others. With regard to state-to-state relations, whisper thoughts suggest to me there is a better way to influence the nations of the world than the policies we have pursued for much of our history. These suggestions include foreign aid, exchange programs, more use of the United Nations, and a greater adherence to international law.

THE WOMEN'S MOVEMENT: AN EVANGELICAL NIGHTMARE

I'm a sixties kid. Like many of my friends at that time, I wanted to make the world a better place. We screamed out against the

31. For a discussion of the attempt of neoconservatives in the Bush administration to create an American empire see, Jentleson, *American Foreign Policy*, 287–90 and Scheer, *Pornography of Power*.

Vietnam War and American militarism. We marched in support of civil rights, environmental protection, and women's rights. Laws were passed in each of these areas to push forward social change. I was proud of the role my generation played in providing the moral energy to pass this important legislation. I brag today that the improved status of women over the last fifty years has been our greatest achievement.

Evangelical Christians had a very different response to the turbulent social change that took place in the 1960s. They raised the battle cry and declared war against the secular humanist tide sweeping the country. Anti-war protests were deeply disturbing to people who revered the military and believed the country only deployed military force when the interests of other countries were at stake. Supreme Court decisions allowing for abortion, and the banning of prayer and Bible reading in the public schools were seen as an attack against the Christian religion. Civil rights legislation and the forced integration of the public schools were viewed as huge government overreach.[32]

The real boogeyman behind the rise of secular culture for evangelicals, however, was the women's movement. As women after World War II started going to college, joining professions, and having fewer babies, militant anti-feminism emerged among evangelical Christians.[33] Women's rights violated several teachings scattered throughout the New Testament. The Bible was seen as inerrant, the bedrock of their religious belief. To question one passage from scripture would place the authority of the Bible in question.

There's a wonderful irony here which the ideological blinders of Christian conservatives prevent them from seeing. Both Jesus and Paul were first-century feminists. In the case of Jesus, as seen from Matthew's Gospel, a woman anoints Jesus at Bethany (26:6–13), women stand by him at the cross in contrast to the disciples

32. An excellent history of the evangelical movement in America can be found in Fitzgerald, *Evangelicals: The Struggle to Shape America.*

33. For a more detailed discussion of the depth of patriarchal values among evangelicals see Du Mez, *Jesus and John Wayne: How Evangelicals Corrupted a Faith and Fractured a Nation.*

who flee (27:55–56), and women play a prominent role at the resurrection (27:61; 28:1–10). The fact that his movement contained single female members was a radical departure with the culture of first-century Palestine (See Luke 8:1–3).

It is more difficult to make this case for Paul because several letters attributed to him contain anti-feminist passages. The most blatant comes in 1 Tim 2:9–15. Here the author of the letter tells women how to dress and forbids them to teach or have authority over a man. With regard to the Adam and Eve story, it was Eve who led Adam astray, but she can redeem herself through childbearing. The author claims to be Paul, but the vast majority of biblical scholars who have addressed the issue argue the letter was written long after Paul had died by someone else. Can you trust the passage in 1 Timothy representing the word of God when it was written by a person who misled readers about authorship?

When I translated chapter 14 in 1 Corinthians from Greek to English for my college professor, it was obvious verses 34 and 35 were a problem. The verses forbid women to speak in church, and, if they have any questions, they are to ask their husbands at home. My professor smiled and claimed verses 34 and 35 were almost certainly inserted by a scribe to bring Paul's message more in line with the culture at the time. Remember, biblical texts in those days were copied by hand by human beings who could add, subtract, or change the meaning of a passage at will.

I was shocked. To defend his statement, my professor showed me how the sentence structure in the two verses was different from Paul's writing style. He then explained that if you take the two inserted verses out of the text the paragraph reads seamlessly. He smiled at me again and said that if he was an English teacher and if a student handed in a paper with such an insertion within a paragraph, he would cut the insertion out of the paper and tell the student the insertion had no logical connection to what the paragraph was about.

Evangelical leaders, who use Paul to support their militant masculine values, conveniently ignore the fact that many leaders in Paul's churches were women. At the conclusion of Romans (see

16:1–16), Paul sends greetings to Phoebe, a church deacon; Prisca, a fellow worker; Tryphaena and Tryphosa, workers in the Lord; and Junia, an apostle. They also ignore one of the most beautiful statements in all of religious literature.

> There can be neither Jew nor Greek, there can be neither slave or freeman, there can be neither male nor female—for you are all one in Christ Jesus. (Gal 3:28)

It gives me goose bumps thinking this statement was made by a first-century man.

Masculine theology has been preached by a wide array of male evangelical leaders of the culture wars that began in the 1980s—James Dobson, Billy and Franklin Graham, Jerry Falwell, Pat Robertson, and Oral Roberts to name a few. Their views were echoed by female counterparts like Phyllis Schlafly, Anita Bryant, and Marabel Morgan whose book *The Total Woman* was a runaway best seller. The book told evangelical women to treat their husbands as a king, tell him he is their hero, stop any nagging, and provide him with plenty of sex so that he remains monogamous. Your place is at home with your children, Morgan counseled her evangelical audience.[34]

These values have had political consequences. Evangelicals by large numbers oppose abortion,[35] birth control, and day care. Women are to stay at home and have babies. The Southern Baptist Convention recently ruled that women cannot be pastors or hold positions of authority over men. Churches led by women are to be purged from the denomination. Men are to lead congregations while women are to serve tea and coffee after the service.

The beautiful statement by Paul quoted above that all are one in Christ almost certainly resulted from Paul being a good listener. His self had been purified by his many deep encounters of divine

34. Morgan, *Total Woman*.

35. There's another wonderful irony here. The Southern Baptist Convention, the flagship organization for evangelical Christians, supported abortion for therapeutic reasons in the early 1950s and 1960s. It was only after pro-choice became a major focus of the feminist movement that they changed tune and joined Roman Catholics in opposing abortion in all or most cases.

love that began on the Damascus Road (see Acts 9:2–7). This purified self allowed whisper thoughts regarding female equality to be received with clarity. Sadly, many evangelicals can't hear that message because their selves are encased by the thick clouds of ideological belief and deep insecurities that need to be purged from their awareness.

THE IMPORTANCE OF GLOBAL GOVERNANCE

When it comes to looking at the world of international politics, all commentators agree it has become global, interdependent, a world where state borders are losing their significance. Trade, the internet, environmental problems, drug trafficking, terrorism, migration, tourism, international finance, American pop culture, biological extinction, and pandemics are some of the forces driving this transformation. While commentators agree on these emerging trends, they disagree on how best to manage the conflict arising from this new international order.

Political realists view the world from the perspective of the nation-state. International politics is a ruthless, dangerous game. Great powers fear and compete with each other. This zero-sum competition creates fear and uncertainty. The best strategy to safely deal with these threats is to increase power, seen primarily as military power. Power is the currency of the international system. This power is wielded by states. Political realists have little interest in international organizations. They manage international conflicts unilaterally with diplomacy first. If diplomacy fails, you replace it with threats of force. War is always on the table as a last resort.

Over the last seventy years a different approach to managing the international system has emerged entitled global governance. Practitioners of this form of statecraft are quick to point out that governance is not world government, a utopian solution with little public support. Instead, proponents of global governance call for international cooperation to build institutions and to support international law as the best approach to managing international conflict.[36]

The number of organizations and institutions created over the last seventy years to manage international conflict and facilitate cooperation between states has been impressive. The premier organization is, of course, the United Nations, which legitimizes multilateral military operations, provides a neutral setting that facilitates diplomacy, promotes peacekeeping to diffuse tense interstate conflict, funds and oversees several important organizations like the World Health Organization and the International Atomic Energy Agency as well as sponsoring important programs for international development, the environment, and public health. The World Trade Organization promotes free trade and provides an arena for dispute resolution. The World Bank provides loans for international development, and the International Monetary Fund works to stabilize currencies. The International Court of Justice and the International Criminal Court function to enforce the rule of international law. Finally, there are a myriad of nongovernmental organizations like Amnesty International, Doctors Without Borders, churches, and foundations that work to ameliorate specific global problems.

To repeat what was said at the outset, global governance is not world government. The world does not have an international police force to maintain law and order, and there are real threats to global world order that need to be addressed. A good example is Russia under Vladimir Putin. The invasions of Georgia in 2008 and the Ukraine in 2014 and 2022 demonstrate a deep dislike for the current international status quo on the part of Russia especially as that status quo relates to the former Soviet empire. In the absence of an international police force, the United States works to protect the territorial integrity of West and East European states through the NATO alliance. Multilateral alliances like NATO are a part of the global governance regime.

36. A good summary of these two approaches to managing conflict in this new international order can be found in Jentleson, *American Foreign Policy*, 287–96.

The best way for the United States to promote global governance is to use the institutions and organizations comprising it more frequently to manage international conflict. While we played a major role in creating these institutions, we have a mixed record when it comes to using them. President George W. Bush unilaterally invaded Iraq in 2003. President Donald Trump prefers to deal with China's violations of international trade agreements on his own rather than taking the dispute to the World Trade Organization.[37] The United States has not ratified the Law of the Sea treaty and has refused to join the International Criminal Court.[38] We can do better!

Foreign policy elites tend to follow one of these two approaches in developing foreign policies for their country based on how they see the world. Those who see the world as a dangerous jungle become political realists who pursue unilateral policies based on a narrow conception of the national interest. Those who see the world as a precious garden pursue multilateral policies that seek to foster international cooperation and the strengthening of the institutions and organizations promoting global governance.

Historically political realism has been a strategy devised by statesmen who feared their country was threatened in an existential way. The reality of the current international system is that the United States faces few credible threats. Our military is more than sufficient to deter any potential aggressor. This military and the accompanying diplomatic strength which follows from it provide us with a unique opportunity to pursue policies that promote global governance. We have tried unilateral hegemony in Iraq as a way to use our power to build an international system in our own image. It has not worked. When I think about all the wars we have fought trying to impose our values on other people and how much devastation has followed from them, love tells me there must be a better way. Maybe if we learn to think globally and work to create an international system that functions to meet the needs of a much larger community we will be more successful. When I ponder the

37. Hu and Spence, "Why Globalization Failed," 54–55.

38. Haass, "World Order 2.0."

challenges that currently face our nation and the world, whisper thoughts message me on the need to support global governance.

THE OHIO TRAIN WRECK

On February 3, 2023, a 150-car Norfolk Southern train traveling from Illinois to Pennsylvania derailed in East Palestine, Ohio, with the result that several cars caught fire and dangerous, toxic chemicals, were released into the air. The National Transportation Safety Board responded immediately, sending a team of investigators to determine what caused the accident and if safety upgrades were warranted. The Environmental Protection Agency, the arm of the government responsible for the release of toxic chemicals and their cleanup, also responded immediately to the dangerous toxic spill.

It is interesting that the two agencies most responsible for dealing with problems such as this are not part of the Department of Transportation. The EPA and the NTSB are both independent agencies. Congress deliberately created the NTSB as separate from the Department of Transportation in order to guarantee unbiased investigations.[39]

These facts about how our government works did not stop several leading Republicans from blasting Secretary of Transportation Pete Buttigieg for being AWOL when it came to this crisis. He has become the most recent lightning rod in right-wing attempts to weaponize the government. The attacks against Buttigieg are part of a broader attempt to criticize the Biden administration and to discredit an openly gay man.

These right-wing Republicans have no interest in some of the inconvenient facts in this case such as the fact that it was the Trump administration that suspended several of the safety regulations that may have prevented the Ohio wreck and that the government agencies primarily responsible for such accidents did respond in a timely manner. As this case shows, democratic government in America has become tribal warfare. The God in

39. Katz, "How Federal Agencies Are Responding."

my life keeps inspiring thoughts that democratic government in this country can't survive this type of incivility in the long run. Most of the politicians who make attacks of this nature claim to be Christian. I often wonder if they ever experience the God of wonder and goodness who inspires these messages to act with civility or whether they miss these messages because their religion is all about ideological belief.

Critics may say that this is merely my partisan voice speaking. I would respond that I get these messages about civility all the time and that Democrats are often responsible for the prompt.

SPINNING OUT

Spinning Out is a Netflix series about the figure skating world. In it Kat, the female lead, is an Olympic hopeful to win a medal in the individual competition. When she receives a serious head injury from a fall on the ice, her world is turned upside down. She contemplates many new avenues for the future, but she ultimately can't leave the skating world. She eventually finds a pair's partner, a much less risky skating event, and the two achieve considerable success together.

The television series portrays much of the less glamorous aspects of the figure skating world. These young athletes make huge sacrifices in their personal life and often suffer serious injury. Even more devastating can be the effect of skating on their family life.

Both parents of the figure skating pair, her mother and his father, pushed their children to satisfy their low self-esteems with dreams of a gold medal. Their love was conditional on performance and remaining committed to a disciplined training regime. Many times throughout the ten episodes of the series I received thoughts that such parenting was wrong. Their children may win a gold medal, but they may never be normal, well-adjusted human beings if they are not loved unconditionally instead of being treated as trophies used to raise parental self-esteem.

I end this chapter on applications with this example to make the point that Whisper Ethics applies to the broad range of

Christian Ethics, not just the relationship between religion and politics. The structure of divine love embedded within the universe provides background music of goodness and love that inspires the whisper thoughts that float through our awareness. It is our responsibility as Christians to listen to these messages and to act on them.

3

Conclusion

Christianity is dying a slow death. This trend is seen most dramatically in Western Europe. Active church membership there as defined by attending church services at least once a month has reached a low of 22 percent.[1] This decline, while less dramatic, has also come to America. A recent poll from the Pew Research Center found 75 percent of Americans declaring themselves as Christian ten years ago, a number that has dropped to 63 percent today.[2]

This decline is especially evident among the younger generation who have come to see Christian belief as unbelievable. The miracle stories, the virgin birth, the physical resurrection of Jesus, and the idea that the world is six thousand years old are just some of the traditional beliefs that no longer make sense to them. The findings of modern science and biblical scholarship have called these traditional beliefs into serious question.

What can save Christianity from this slow death that appears to be taking place? My recommendation is for a new focus away

1. Tornieli, "Statistics on the Slow Evaporation of European Christianity."
2. Schaeffer, "Striking Findings for 2021."

from what Christians believe to what they do.[3] It's time we recognize what Jesus' major concern was. His goal was not salvation in heaven but bringing in the kingdom of God to earth. That would happen when politics was governed by love and concern for one's neighbor. He instructed his close followers to pray for such an outcome.

> Our Father in heaven, may your name be held holy, your kingdom come, your will be done, on earth as in heaven.
> Matthew 6: 9–10

Pay attention to what so many of you pray each Sunday. You are asking God to bring his kingdom to earth where it will be governed like affairs in heaven. Though many Christians have misinterpreted it, the book of Revelation makes the same point. It's not about leaving the world and going to heaven but rather about bringing God's rule to earth.[4]

Let's assume Jesus was right and the Lord's Prayer expresses God's intention for us to bring his kingdom to earth. The question then becomes "how do we get there? How do we bring the kingdom of heaven to earth?" In the introduction, I argued the Bible was not very helpful in this regard.

To review briefly, biblical passage-picking can be used to support any political position one chooses to take. We can use passage-picking to encourage a Christian to take a particular stance on a political issue or to suggest that God is behind the advocate's position, a rather arrogant assumption to say the least, but passage-picking cannot explain how a person actually decides a political issue.

Whisper Ethics helps to solve that problem. It explains how humans decide on the issues governing their lives which includes politics. We make decisions to act by responding to thoughts that float through our awareness. We can choose to decide for God or our self-centered interests. By cleaning the windows surrounding one's self, Whisper Ethics also provides the tools to enable

3. This is the major theme of my book *Moving Beyond Belief.* It's a theme that has even been taken up by some evangelicals. See Warren, *Purpose Driven Life.*

4. See Bart Ehrman's excellent commentary on this often misunderstood book, *Armageddon: What the Bible Really Says About the End.*

Christians to do a better job deciding for God and living the teachings of Jesus. Most important, Whisper Ethics puts God in charge of our ethical decision-making. We act in the world as Christians not because the Bible tells us so but because we are responding to thoughts inspired by God that gently flow through our awareness. The only note of caution regarding this approach to ethical decision making is that we make an honest effort to only respond to messages that ask us to move beyond our narrow self-interests.

Many Christians like to point out their religion does not apply to politics. Instead, it's all about belief in Jesus Christ as their savior. I have both heard and read debates on the subject. For me, the answer is quite clear as the applications in the last chapter suggest. God is the one inspiring me with thoughts to apply my religion to politics. As a Christian, I am called to take these whisper thoughts seriously.

I can't think of a more important time to work with God in bringing in her kingdom. Nuclear war threatens human life on the planet with extinction. Climate change poses a similar threat over the course of the next one hundred years. Marked income inequality, racial exclusion, and a tribal political mentality which lacks civility and a sense of the common good threaten the existence of the democratic government which has made America such a special place to live.

Critics who read this book will say there is nothing new here. This book could have been written by a staff member of the Democratic National Committee. My response to such criticism is quite simple. Let's assume that love is part of the created universe and that God is somehow behind it. Let's further assume that Paul learned something about this love from his many encounters with God that are well documented in Acts and his letters. In chapter 13 of 1 Corinthians he reports to us what he has learned.

> Love is always patient and kind; love is never jealous; love is not boastful or conceited, it is never rude and never seeks its own advantage, it does not take offence or store up grievances. Love does not rejoice in wrongdoing, but it finds its joy in the truth. It is always ready to

> make allowances, to trust, to hope and to endure whatever comes. (1 Cor 13:4–7)

If what Paul says about love in the passage above is an accurate statement about some of the characteristics that flow from love, use your reason to apply these characteristics to some of the political issues raised in the last chapter. I suspect you will come to many of the same positions I did because the love I sense in my life is the same love Paul encountered in the later stages of his adult life.

If you need further confirmation, read the Sermon on the Mount in Matthew (chapters 5–7). Jesus receives whisper thoughts asking him to apply love, a love that reconciles one with their enemies and insists on looking out for the needs of others, to everyday situations that occur in life. The standard is set very high. Living love involves more than obeying rules. You must become infused with the spirit of love that undergirds the rules. Yes, you must not kill, but hating your neighbor is just as bad. The God who inspired Jesus with whisper thoughts two thousand years ago is the same God that messages me. The main difference between the two of us is the self. The windows of his perception were much cleaner than mine.

As I pointed out introducing Whisper Ethics, humans are decision makers. We make choices. Our choices reflect the thoughts floating through our awareness. We can choose from thoughts reflecting off of God's goodness and love or those stemming from an egocentric perspective. It is important to note that our choices matter.

My friend Jeffrey Frantz has written an important article entitled "What We Do and Say Matters."[5] Every action we take, no matter how small, has consequences. The world of quantum physics is a strange one. At the subatomic level everything is connected. Reality at its most basic level is an interconnected web which means that even a miniscule change somewhere has consequences everywhere. Nothing is inconsequential.

Take, for example, the problem of climate change. According to Frantz, an ethics of consequences asks us to do the right thing

5. Frantz, "What We Do and Say Matters."

because our actions matter. We cannot avoid our responsibility on this issue by saying it's the government's problem to solve or the fault of a rapidly growing Chinese economy. We need to take actions of our own because our choices matter.

Because everything at the base of reality is connected, a simple thing as turning off the lights reverberates throughout the universe. Hanging out the laundry, raising the temperature in the house during summer and relying more on fans to provide comfort, eating less meat, slowing your driving speed on major highways, purchasing an electric vehicle, and installing solar panels all contribute to the fight against climate change. To not make such choices contributes to the dangerous problem that threatens the very survival of the planet.

There are times during the day when a dark cloud descends over my awareness. I think we are losing the fight against climate change, Russia and China are military rivals with a deep dislike of the current status quo within the international system, and the health of American democracy hangs in the balance. But then the cloud lifts, and I sense this wonderful presence of goodness and love. I can't shut it off. It keeps returning. As I continue my daily meditative practice to help deal with my psychological junk, this loving presence grows stronger.

At the outset of this essay, I stated my lifelong goal was to do a better job living the teachings of Jesus. Those teachings call on us to work to bring in the kingdom of God, and I want to conclude with the idea that this is not some utopian dream. Billions of people around the globe receive the same revelatory experiences I do. Against this loving backdrop, whisper thoughts float through their awareness calling on them to act in ways that go beyond their self-centered interests.

Imagine if billions of people focused better attention on these whisper thoughts and acted on them. Even small acts of kindness and love will have an impact throughout the planet. As John Forbes Nash tells us, we can choose the voice we listen to and organize our life around. By listening to and acting on the whisper thoughts that reflect off of the goodness and love embedded within life, we will be working with God to make the world a better place. I can think of no greater honor than to align myself with God in this way.

Bibliography

Allison, Graham, and Zelikow, Philip. *Essence of Decision: Explaining the Cuban Missile Crisis*. New York: Bloomsbury, 1999.

Bergon, Frank. "Guns and Grammar, or How to Read the Second Amendment." *Los Angeles Review of Books*, Jul 2, 2023.

Bowman, Tom. "Reagan Guided Huge Buildup in Arms Race." *Baltimore Sun*, Jun 8, 2004.

Buber, Martin. *I and Thou*. New York: Scribner, 1970.

Caporal, Jack. "Average Net Worth of Americans by Age, Education, and Race." *The Motley Fool*, Feb 28, 2022. https://www.fool.com/research/average-net-worth-americans/.

Carrington, Damian. "Gulf Stream Could Collapse as Early as 2025, Study Suggests." *The Guardian*, Jul 25,2023.

Carroll, James. *Constantine's Sword: The Church and the Jews*. New York: Houghton and Mifflin, 2001.

CNN Staff. "Trump Dashed Dreams of Reform in Iran: The Country's New Hardline President is Living Proof." Jun 20, 2021. https://www.cnn.com/2021/06/20/middleeast/iran-analysis-trump-raisi-cmd-intl/index.html.

Damasio, Antonio. *Decartes' Error: Emotion, Reason and the Human Brain*. New York: Penguin, 2005.

Ehrman, Bart D. *Armageddon: What the Bible Really Says About the End*. New York: Simon and Schuster, 2023.

Ellsberg, Daniel. *The Doomsday Machine: Confessions of a Nuclear War Planner*. New York: Bloomsbury, 2017.

Fitzgerald, Frances. *The Evangelicals: The Struggle to Shape America*. New York: Simon and Schuster, 2017.

Frankl, Viktor E. *Man's Search for Meaning*. Boston: Beacon, 1959.

Frantz, Jeffrey E. *The God You Didn't Know You Could Believe In*. Haworth, NY: St. Johann, 2020.

———. "What We Do and Say Matters." ProgressiveChristianity.org, Jul 12, 2023. https://progressivechristianity.org/resources/what-we-do-and-say-matters/.

Grudem, Wayne. *Politics According to the Bible*. Grand Rapids: Zondervan, 2010.

Haass, Richard. "World Order 2.0." *Foreign Affairs* 96.1 (Jan/Feb 2017) 2–9.

Hauerwas, Stanley. *The Peaceable Kingdom: A Primer in Christian Ethics*. Notre Dame, IN: Notre Dame University Press, 1991.

Herrick, Rick. *Moving Beyond Belief: A New Focus for the Christian Faith*. Eugene, OR: Wipf and Stock, 2022.

Hu, Fred, and Spence, Michael. "Why Globalization Stalled and How to Restart It." *Foreign Affairs* 96.4 (Jul/Aug 2017) 54–63.

Jentleson, Bruce W. *American Foreign Policy: The Dynamics of Choice in the 21st Century*. New York: W. W. Norton and Company, 2013.

Katz, Eric. "How Federal Agencies Are Responding to the Toxic Train Derailment in Ohio." Government Executive, Feb 14, 2023. https://www.govexec.com/management/2023/02/federal-agencies-responding-toxic-train-derailment-ohio/382955/.

Le Doux, Joseph. *Synaptic Self: How Our Brains Become Who We Are*. New York: Penguin, 2003.

Levin, Dov H. *Meddling in the Ballot Box: The Causes and Effects of Partisan Electoral Interventions*. London: Oxford University Press, 2020.

Lindsey, Rebecca and Dahlman, Luann. "Climate Change: Global Temperature." NOAA Climate.gov, Jan 18, 2023. https://www.climate.gov/news-features/understanding-climate/climate-change-global-temperature.

"Mass Shootings in the United States: Statistics and Facts." Statista Research Department, May 16, 2023. https://www.statista.com.topics>10843.

Meacham, Jon. *And There Was Light: Abraham Lincoln and the American Struggle*. New York: Random House, 2022.

Miller, Cassie, and Kieffer, Caleb, "Hate and Extremism in the Mainstream and on the Main Street," Southern Poverty Law Center, Annual Report, 2022 edition.

Morgan, Marabel. *The Total Woman: How to Make Your Marriage Come Alive!* Chicago: F. H. Revell, 1973.

Nasar, Sylvia. *A Beautiful Mind*. New York: Simon and Schuster, 2011.

Pauly, Reid. "Remembering the Prague Speech." The Ploughshares Fund, Apr 5, 2011. https://www.ploughshares.org/issues-analysis/article/remembering-prague-speech.

Pinker, Steven. *The Better Angels of Our Nature: Why Violence Has Declined*. New York: Penguin, 2012.

Plomin, Robert. *Blueprint: How DNA Makes Us Who We Are*. London: Penguin, 2018.

Price, Carter C. and Edwards, Kathryn A. "Trends in Income From 1975–2018." The Rand Corporation. https://www.rand.org/pubs/working-papers/WRA 516-11.html.

Schaeffer, Katherine. "Striking Features for 2021." Pew Research Center, December 17, 2021. https://www.pewresearch.org/fact-tank/2021/12/17/striking-findings-from-2021/

Scheer, Robert. *The Pornography of Power: How Defense Hawks Hijacked 9/11 and Weakened America.* New York: Hachette Books Group, 2008.

Smith, Peter H. *Talons of the Eagle: Dynamics of U.S.-Latin American Relations.* New York: Oxford University Press, 2000.

Tian, Nan, et al. "Trends in World Military Expenditure, 2021," Stockholm Peace Research Institute, April 2022.

Tornielli, Andrea. "The Statistics on the Slow Evaporation of European Christianity." Mercator.net, May 30, 2018. https://mercatornet.com/the-statistics-on-the-slow-evaporation-of-european-christianity/23242/.

Torreon, Barbara Salazar, and Plagakis, Sofia. "Instances of Use of United States Armed Forces Abroad, 1798–2022." Congressional Research Service. https://crsreports.congress.gov/product/pdf/R/R42738.

Vines, David. "The Pentagon's New Generation of Secret Military Bases." Mother Jones, April 29, 2020.

Ward, Jon. "Radical Beliefs in Spiritual Warfare Played a Major Role in Jan. 6, an Expert Argues." Yahoo News, Feb 16, 2023. https://news.yahoo.com/radical-beliefs-in-spiritual-warfare-played-a-major-role-in-jan-6-an-expert-argues-100039606.html.aI1ROcHM6Ly93d3cuZ29vZ2xlLmNvbS8&gucc_referrer_sig=AQAAAJmjvgd5QgdNqWnXZb3JH93JIF40eJxao1twfgxjEwpVJJvDdGkNAimZA8PxWPHibwKWA06qdsuIjEc33TTGHfTvQvtrguzGX5t9duzft13QIeiSZACmrG719R3NOZxVs3Nq3VuCG70PO5Xmw8SJEspCOFVcQ3ZUotzarzV2jGT9

Warren, Rick. *The Purpose Driven Life: What on Earth Am I Here For?* Grand Rapids, MI: Zondervan, 2013.

Wallis, Jim. *God's Politics: Why the Right Gets It Wrong.* New York: Harper Collins, 2006.

"What Happened to Mahsa Zhina Amini?" Amnesty International, Sep 15, 2023. https://www.amnesty.org/en/latest/news/2023/09/what-happened-to-mahsa-zhina-amini/.

Wikipedia, the Free Online Encyclopedia, Wikipedia.org.

"World Military Spending Passes $2 Trillion for First Time." Stockholm International Peace Research Institute, Apr 25, 2022. https://www.sipri.org/media/press-release/2022/world-military-expenditure-passes-2-trillion-first-time.

Printed in the USA
CPSIA information can be obtained
at www.ICGtesting.com
LVHW010747270224
772875LV00003B/24